C000093307

#LivingTheDream
Nine women share the emotional
and practical realities
of life away from 'home'

Written by Adrienne Walder, Annabel Cotton,
Avivit Delgoshen, Deborah Gray, Carrie Frais,
Elizabeth Heath, Jane Mitchell, Morag Makey
and Sue Wilson

With commentary from psychotherapist Leigh Matthews

Edited by Carrie Frais

First edition published in 2020 by MumAbroad SL

This edition published in Great Britain by Springtime Books

© MumAbroad, 2021

All rights reserved. No part of this publication may be reproduced, stored in or introduced into a retrieval system or transmitted, in any form, or by any means (electronic, mechanical, photocopying, recording or otherwise) without the prior written permission from the publisher.

This book is sold subject to the condition that it shall not, by way of trade or otherwise, be lent, resold, hired out or otherwise circulated without the publisher's prior consent in any form of binding or cover other than in which it is published and without a similar condition including this condition being imposed on the subsequent purchaser.

ISBN: 978-1-8381746-7-5

Cover and interior designed by David Nebot.

What people are saying about #LivingTheDream…

Divorce, death, alcoholism… these are women's real stories about what lies beneath the Facebook veneer of life abroad. They may be a harsh wake-up call in many cases, but their stories are also refreshing, uplifting and beautifully told.
**Zoe Dare Hall,
Sunday Times**

A great strength of this book is that it avoids most of the clichés that surround those who relocate. In several places it confronts them face on to dispel fanciful dreams and watery eyed romantic projections of Europe as a land of sunny, easy plenty.
Brett Hetherington

I couldn't put this book down! Each of the nine stories is so beautifully and honestly written. Filled with anecdotes and wisdom from unique lives with one thing in common: the experience of living abroad. Every story is told with a unique, strong voice, through an individual and fascinating lens. Having grown up bilingual and moving between multiple countries, I can relate to so many of the dilemmas and challenges faced by each of the women in the book.
Dulcet Wanderlust

Many of us dream of making the move - reading these tales gives the good and the bad experiences. The risks, the highs and the lows and what it's really like navigating the every day when there's a language or cultural barrier. Quite addictive,

you'll want to plough on through and learn more.
Catrin Macdonnell

You can only admire their openness and honesty. It made me want to meet all of them over a long, sun-soaked lunch somewhere, to hear more!
Victoria Smith

The waves of each story rise & fall differently. If you're not an expat, and think the life is always better on the other side - well, this will give you real insight into the highs and lows of a "lucky" life away from home.
EdenMama

This is a great read, part advert for the wonders of travel and uprooting yourself from everything that's familiar and part warning about what you might miss.
Anonymous

Their resilience through their struggles and their determination to continue in the lives that they have chosen really come across.
C Imrie

The fact that these challenges all stemmed from their expat experiences made for a very different take on life. Expat or not - this is a book that celebrates all types of women.
Jane Garrard

As an expat living in Spain for 14 years, this book resonates in a way that other accounts don't. It speaks to the slices of life, good and bad, that people don't think or talk about enough, when they envision living abroad and it hit home in a very powerful and real way.
Sam Mednick

This book reads as if you were sitting at a table with these nine very different women, each telling their own story in a very personal and sometimes intimate way, sometimes so touchingly and openly.
Rinus

Beyond life in foreign lands, the book really touches on so many of the universal worries and questions about life we all carry with us. An uplifting and inspiring read.
JC Andreu

A wonderful honest, human and personal collection of stories. A gem of a book.
Simon M

Many at 'home' may compare a move to the 2 or 3 weeks spent 'on holiday' and believe that we get all the best bits, and none of the challenges, of life away. These stories bring you a sense that distance from family, the need to find work, creating new networks and friendships and staying sane high amongst the challenges which we face. And whilst there are challenges, the life in a new country, integration, bringing up second, and sometimes third culture kids and expanding our cultural awareness does in the end make it worth #livingthedream.
Ali Meehan

Contents

*This compilation of stories is dedicated to my mum and dad,
and to everyone's parents who have gifted
their children roots and wings.*

Introduction

I dislike the word 'expat' but, for simplicity, the term has been used in this introduction and in some of our stories. It would be better to describe me and my fellow writers as 'immigrants temporarily or permanently residing in a country other than the one in which they were raised'. Unfortunately, that's a bit of a mouthful. The word 'expat' has probably now run its course, as it retains connotations of privileged, financially mobile western white men and women working abroad, or retirees relaxing on sun-soaked beaches. Nowadays, people are choosing to emigrate for a myriad of different reasons and some of us feel that being labelled an expat can set us apart from our adopted cultures when, in fact, we are trying to do exactly the opposite.

The women who have contributed to this collection of stories all share the (often) rollercoaster experience of moving away from the country of their birth. Not all of us actively decided to move to another country, however, as you will find out. Moving abroad can be exciting, stimulating, enthralling and glamorous (the latter less often than you might think). We are sometimes viewed as courageous, uprooting ourselves from the security blanket of having one's extended family nearby to face new adventures and experiences in far-flung corners of the world.

#Blessed   #WishYouWereHere   #LivingTheDream. Right?

Yet, our lives – like anyone else's – can be emotional, confusing and challenging. We sometimes find ourselves victims of 'toxic positivity', when people tell us how 'lucky' we are because our lifestyle is coveted, which can undermine some of our day-to-day struggles and life-changing moments. When we experience anxiety, stress, insomnia, loneliness, fear or even depression caused by, amongst other things, culture shock, rootlessness, social exclusion, grief or bureaucracy, we struggle with people's perceptions versus our own reality.

Most of us do our best to 'fit in', to communicate and present ourselves as effectively as possible in the face of cultural challenges and language barriers. Friendships that take years to cement are lost as people come, and then go. The concept of 'home' and 'belonging' is a constant conversation.

We received an overwhelmingly positive response to the book's first edition, as can be seen in our reviews. Many of the chapters had been written during or soon after some fairly challenging (at best) or traumatic (at worst) events and so, a year on, we felt the need to add both measured reflection and analysis, which contrast with the often raw emotion of each individual's story. Following each chapter are the author's 'Reflections' - what we have all learnt from our experiences and some words of wisdom with the beauty of hindsight. After our 'Reflections', we find out 'What the Expert Says' - beautifully written, insightful analysis on each writer's unique experience from Barcelona-based Australian psychologist Leigh Matthews, a specialist in the challenges faced by those of us living away from home.

This collection of narratives is not a cry for sympathy. We are all responsible for the decisions we make in life and, overall, most of us are very content with the lives that we are living. But, we are not always 'Living the Dream'. I felt a need to unravel the reality of life away from 'home' for what it really is and to dispel some of the 'rose-tinted' perceptions. We are real people facing real challenges in the real world. Just sometimes, when you want to put your head in the sand, the beach is only around the corner.

We hope you enjoy our stories.

Carrie

Thank you...

...to my inspirational fellow writers, Adrienne, Annabel, Avivit, Deborah, Elizabeth, Jane, Morag and Sue, who kindly let me persuade them to tell their powerful stories,

...to Leigh Matthews, who went above and beyond my expectations with her invaluable input, wisdom and sound advice on each of our writers' experiences,

...to Jo Parfitt & Jack Scott at Summertime Publishing for their expertise, knowledge and guidance helping me craft this new version of #LivingTheDream,

...to Monica Kruger and Catriona Groves who have spent hours proofreading the texts,

...to Jonathan de Mounteney for his patience when explaining copyright and royalty issues,

...to David Nebot, whose design skills I hope will help give the women behind this narrative the shiny platform they deserve,

...and lastly thank you to Tom, Poppy & Bertie who have given me love, support and stability in this ever-changing world.

Introducing our expert

LEIGH MATTHEWS
AUSTRALIAN REGISTERED PSYCHOLOGIST

B.A. Psychology (Hons), USYD; Post Grad Cert. Psych Practice, ACAP; MAPS; AHPRA PSY0000965562

Leigh Matthews moved to Barcelona in 2011 after falling for her Catalan husband in 2010. Following a successful private practice in Brisbane, Australia, she founded Therapy in Barcelona in December 2011. Leigh worked solo as she raised her son following his birth in November 2012. With the 2018 expansion into a group practice, Therapy in Barcelona embraced more clients and an international team of therapists. Run by internationals for internationals, the centre specialises in the complexities expat life can bring to adults, couples, kids, teens and families. Leigh is happily in the trenches with her clients, therapists, and expat women and running toward all the scourges and graces of life abroad.

CHAPTER
ONE

Calling 'Time' on Drinking Culture

ADRIENNE WALDER
MID LEVELS (HONG KONG)

Adrienne Walder, 48
Graham Street, Hong Kong

Photo by CANTONBROS

Adrienne Walder spent her formative years in London scaling the career ladder at notorious multi-national advertising agencies during the day and descending into London's finest drinking establishments by night. After 10 years, she was looking for a quieter life and moved to Hamble, a sailing village on England's South Coast, where she enjoyed a slightly slower paced life. After meeting her husband and following their unsuccessful quest to become parents, they swapped the muted streetlights of their sleepy Hampshire village for the omnipresent neon glow of Hong Kong in 2013. These days Adrienne works as an English teacher and is often found out on the waters around Hong Kong, accompanied by an ice cold soda water.

Calling 'Time' on Drinking Culture

In 2012 my husband, David, and I divulged to our friends that we were relocating from the UK to Hong Kong. The riposte from one of my cousins etched itself uncomfortably into my mind. "You'll fit perfectly into the expat partying lifestyle", she said. The inference, that I was a 'seasoned lush', jarred. However, despite feeling judged, I knew she was probably right. My husband and I were party people, who rarely survived a weekend without an accompanying hangover and we were more often than not, the last ones to leave any party, thanks to our voracious fear of missing out. From my past brief experience of working in Hong Kong, I knew it was a mecca for those who lived their lives by the 'work hard, play hard' mantra, and that was us in a nutshell. The last thing I could have ever expected was that moving to Hong Kong would result in me becoming a non-drinker and vocal advocate for sobriety.

The catalyst for taking the plunge to uproot our lives from the UK to Hong Kong had been our unsuccessful quest to start a family. We had been snared in a vicious cycle of the thrill of falling pregnant, the trauma of miscarrying and the ensuing pain, which we would numb with alcohol. After four agonising miscarriages, each one taking a greater toll on my mental health than the previous one, my husband and I arrived at the conclusion that we didn't want children enough to continue along that torturous path. Almost as soon as we made the decision, David was offered an exciting job opportunity in Asia and it felt as though fate was taking us by the hand and guiding us gently away from the previous couple of years' anguish. We leapt at the chance to pursue a new adventure, which seemed totally feasible now that a future starring just the two of us was a certainty.

I genuinely thought I would slot seamlessly into Hong Kong life having lived and worked in London for many years and being accustomed to big city living – and in some ways I did. I pretty much exited the aeroplane and entered the buzzing Soho bars in time for happy hour – enjoying my first lychee martini within hours of setting foot in Hong Kong. I connected with old colleagues and friends of friends, who had moved to the city, to lay the foundations for burgeoning friendships. I hit the ground running in my quest to find a job and thanks to some intense networking, I very quickly got offered a position within a well-known PR agency. Everything was working out just perfectly… until I started working.

The job was an unmitigated disaster and I was totally unsuited to the role, the company culture and the unrelenting workload. For those first couple of months my evenings were spent self-medicating in the countless bars with my husband and an array of superficial friends. As my workload increased, so did my stress levels. I stopped sleeping, stopped eating, felt completely ill-equipped to cope with anything in my life and was constantly in tears. When we received news that one of our closest friends at home had breast cancer, I felt helpless, inconsolable without my regular support network by my side and completely adrift. To top it all, my intense stress and anxiety unleashed all the trauma from my miscarriages, which I had buried and never allowed myself to process at the time. I was completely overwhelmed. One evening as I looked out of our 15th floor window and contemplated the possibility of jumping to remove all the pain, I woke up to just how desperate things had become. The next day I saw a doctor and was signed off work with situational depression and anxiety. I never went back to that job.

This was a turning point for my life in Hong Kong. I signed up to do a TESOL (teaching English as a second language) course to give myself a bit of breathing space, while I worked out if I wanted to return to agency life. I excelled on the course, discovering I was a natural teacher and it started to restore my confidence. After a few false starts, I got a job in a wonderful kindergarten, teaching English, and I've never gone back to my old career. With the help of counselling, I was able to address many of the issues that had seeded my breakdown. As I got mentally stronger, I felt better equipped to start forging new meaningful friendships. And as stability was resumed, I was ready to embrace everything living in Asia could offer me.

The following four years David and I fitted perfectly into the expat party lifestyle, just as my cousin predicted. We are both keen sailors and we became regular crew on a yacht, spending most weekends growing and cementing new friendships on-board with a can of Tsing Tao (local beer), glass of Prosecco or rum and coke constantly fixed in our hands. As our friendship group expanded, so did our social lives. We attended: lavish balls; dinners at private members' clubs and fine dining restaurants; boozy brunches; casual barbecues; gala dinners; house parties; music festivals; the Hong Kong Rugby Sevens; the Happy Valley horse racing; raucous karaoke sing-offs; and a seemingly never-ending slew of fancy dress parties. We partied in the streets of Lan Kwai Fung clutching syringes filled with vodka jello, we propped up the bars of Soho while imbibing an endless stream of espresso martinis and we occasionally found ourselves leaving nightclubs in daylight as others were just starting their days. When we needed a respite from Hong Kong, we ventured to the tranquil paradise of Palawan, the casinos of Macau, the hustle and bustle of Bangkok, the surface-deep perfection of Singapore, the weird tropical haven of Sanya, the serene beauty of the Mekong Delta, or the ramshackle charm of Siem Reap – among others. Everywhere we went and everything we did, we were accompanied by booze.

Despite having many crazily fun experiences fuelled by alcohol, over time I was finding that the ensuing hangovers were becoming less and less manageable. I would write-off frequent Sundays because I was incapable of moving from the sofa, causing me to become engulfed with guilt for wasting my life away. Although my partying was always firmly scheduled for the weekends, the after effects were increasingly spilling over into the working week. The start of the week was often heralded with a black cloud of depression, pounding anxiety and an inefficiently-functioning, woolly brain. The post drinking comedown was starting to outweigh the drinking high.

In Hong Kong, alcohol is accessible 24/7 and 'problem' drinking is normalised, spawning a blurred line between socially acceptable drinking and addiction. Nevertheless, I was uncomfortably aware that I was not as in control of my drinking as I wanted to be. I could not predict when I would be able to moderate or when the wheels would fall off and I would wake up the following morning with my memories erased, doused in paranoia, shame and self-loathing. Gradually it was dawning on me that my relationship with alcohol was becoming quite dangerous.

I never hit the fabled rock bottom of: coming to in a police cell; waking up in a hospital bed with no recollection of how I'd got there; needing a drink first thing in the morning to fix my DTs (alcohol withdrawal); or destroying my marriage and friendships. I was a grey area drinker, occupying the murky space between the extremes of rock bottom and the occasional tipple, and constantly wrestling with concerns surrounding my drinking habits. I no longer wanted to see how far I could push things and it was clear that I needed to do something before I slipped down a more self-destructive path. I decided to take a trial break and I successfully stopped drinking for seven and a half weeks.

During that time I noticed many dramatic changes, the most notable being that my mental health took a significant U-turn – my anxiety, anger and pessimism were replaced with contentment and positivity. My energy levels increased, I started sleeping really well, my face started to glow and I lost weight. However, December arrived with the usual onslaught of Christmas party invitations and the temptation of festive boozing proved too much and I picked up the bottle again. I was astounded at how quickly I fell back into my binge-drinking ways and undid all the good of the previous weeks. After a booze-infused Christmas break, I felt bloated, depressed and disgusted with myself and I resolved to make alcohol-free living a permanent fixture in my life.

Rather than debating this huge life change with anyone, I wrote a cathartic 'goodbye letter' to alcohol and posted it on my blog, averting the prospect of being talked out of giving up. I expected a few family members and close friends to read it: to help them to understand why I was making this choice; to save me from the tedium of repeating my reasons over and over again; and to make it harder for me to back down from this decision. Much to my surprise, the blog went viral and I realised just how many of us were struggling in silence with our grey area drinking.

David's reaction to the blog took me aback. He was furious that I hadn't thought to discuss such a monumental decision with him before announcing it to the world. I saw his point. I suspect he was also as fearful as I was about how a relationship that had been built on a mutual love of revelry could survive with one of us abstaining. I reassured him that I would still go out and party, while internally grappling with the terror that no one would want to party with sober me and I would never again have the confidence to hit the dance floor, belt out karaoke or engage a group with my quick-witted repartee. However, my fear of the corrosive consequences of continuing drinking eclipsed my concerns about stopping.

I focused all of my energy into quitting drinking. I devoured self-help books about moving to an alcohol-free existence and autobiographies by people who had turned their lives around as a result of stopping. For the first couple of months, I kept a fairly low profile, retreating socially, to keep temptation at bay, which was relatively easy during those quieter winter months. By the time the weather got warmer and our social lives picked up again, I was spurred on to continue, because of the positive changes to my mental health. I no longer felt anxious and the vicious negative chatter in my head had been quelled. Without my gloomy internal running commentary I was starting to radiate happiness and calm. David started to notice the benefits of living with a more emotionally balanced, less angry wife.

With the absence of hangovers, I gained time to reignite old interests and I filled my spare time with painting, singing, sailing, reading, diving, writing, hiking and swimming – meeting new friends in the process. My life started to brim with activities that nurtured my soul and injected worth to my being. David joined me in many of these activities and our time together started to hold more substance and significance than propping up a bar numbing the stresses of everyday life.

Sober holidays were a complete revelation. They switched from being all about the night-time antics to being all about the daytime action. Unexpectedly, I found myself seeking out activities to fill my days, rather than shifting from my bed to a sun lounger. Holidays were no longer an excuse for over-indulgence, letting loose and partying. Instead they were far more enjoyable, fulfilling and restful when the days were filled with diving, swimming, hiking, cycling and exploring. Even my husband relished the benefits of this different style holiday and we now lean towards calmer destinations, where we can try out different activities and be tucked up in bed before midnight.

While there were many benefits of stopping drinking, I did experience some difficulties by going against the cultural norm. Some of my friendships that had been forged over bottles of wine fell by the wayside. Maybe my quitting had placed the spotlight on their relationship with alcohol and it made them uncomfortable or maybe we simply had little else in common to sustain the friendship. There were other friends, who were absolutely fine with me being alcohol-free on the whole. Yet, on nights out as they got increasingly drunk, they clearly found my sobriety awkward and would actively avoid me, leaving me feeling like the unpopular kid at school observing them from the periphery. I found that very hurtful.

It took quite some time to get used to sober socialising and to understand which situations I could cope with and which I couldn't. Gatherings in Hong Kong's bars or restaurants where it was easy to talk to people worked, whereas those where I was crammed into a packed, noisy bar full of drunk people, absolutely did not. I have never been very good at working a roomful of strangers and I used to rely heavily on the false confidence given to me by alcohol to prop me up in those kinds of situations. As a result, I found parties where I knew a large proportion of the guests preferable to deal with than those where I only knew a few. Most importantly, I realised that I needed to have an escape route planned so I could extract myself when the booze kicked in and people started repeating themselves, saying things they would never say sober, getting confrontational or just stopped making sense.

By removing alcohol from my life, I had also erased my go-to coping mechanism. Eight months into quitting drinking, adversity struck, when David's drink was spiked on a night out and we had over US$10,000 stolen from our bank account. Worryingly, this is a fairly common crime in Hong Kong, with mainly male Westerners being the target. The perpetrator spikes their victim's drink with either Rohypnol or GHB, causing them to become disorientated, to lower their inhibitions and to have memory blackouts. While under the influence of these drugs, victims are induced to go to ATM machines and to withdraw cash that they unknowingly hand over to the criminals. The default daily withdrawal sum for many bank accounts in Hong Kong is set at around US$10,000, and many account holders are totally unaware of this. This makes this crime particularly prevalent in Hong Kong. Victims often only realise they have been targeted and robbed when checking their bank accounts the next day, by which time the drugs have left their system.

Many of the victims are so ashamed about what has happened that they never report the crime and I suspect David would have preferred to have taken that route. However, I pushed him to go to the police and to try to recover the money through our bank. It took a number of weeks for our bank to even provide us with the details of the ATMs from which the money had been withdrawn, and then for the police to be provided with the footage from the ATMs. In the footage, only David could be seen withdrawing the cash – the perpetrator being wise enough to know how to stay out of view – and the police instructed us to stop trying to recover the money through our bank or we would be prosecuted for fraud.

It was a horrific situation in terms of the large sum of money that was unrecoverable, and the terror that David had been taken advantage of in such a way. During that time, there was nothing I wanted to do more than to drown myself in wine rather than living with the trauma and fear of what had, and what could have, happened. Nevertheless, we got through the ordeal and I realised that as painful as it was to have to live the nightmare in sharp focus, it also meant that I was forced to process and deal with it in the moment. This was the first time I had had to draw on a coping mechanism that didn't come from a bottle. I started to see how it was possible to handle torment and move on quickly.

This situation also forced David to evaluate his relationship with alcohol. He was extremely shaken up by what had happened to him and for allowing himself to become vulnerable to such a crime. He started to temper his intake and reign in his impulse to chase the party until the bitter end. He started to fill his time by going to the gym, playing tennis and looking after himself better. Both of us were now leading less chaotic lives and were looking and feeling much better for it.

Not drinking alcohol has now become completely normal to me. By overhauling my life in such a dramatic way, I have learnt so much more about myself. I am not the 'extroverted' party girl I thought I was. I have discovered that the real me is actually quite introverted, shy and self-conscious, until I feel comfortable with people. I don't enjoy being in large groups, I am much more content socialising with a small posse of friends. I love my own company and in fact I really need time on my own to recharge. I'm far more fulfilled and content with the less hectic, more peaceful life I live these days, without alcohol stirring up trouble.

For 30 years, I was utterly captivated by alcohol and I wasted so much time with my head buried in the sand, slowly breaking myself by believing that it added value to my life. Over those years it slowly stole my confidence and my self-respect. Since quitting I have emerged from a slightly fragile and brittle shell and evolved into someone strong, self-assured and courageous. I had had glimpses of that person over the years but alcohol had muted her by welcoming in self-doubt, fear and shame. Now, I am content to be me, I am proud to be me and I like myself. I have discovered a confidence I never believed I was capable of feeling and I will happily put myself into situations that previously would have felt totally out of my reach. I feel far less insignificant now and I exude an aura of calm and strength that I never had previously. I think people are more drawn to me as a result.

If someone had told me when I left for Hong Kong all those years ago, that I would become a non-drinker while living here, I would have laughed and thought "how boring!" Now I know that sobriety is far from dull. Sobriety has drawn back the curtains and thrown open the windows to a glorious, bright future, filled with possibilities. My only regret is that I waited so long to pluck up the courage to take that first tentative peek outside.

REFLECTIONS

Calling 'Time' on Drinking Culture

by ADRIENNE WALDER

Quitting drinking is without question one of my greatest achievements but it has not been easy. This is the advice I would give to anyone questioning their drinking habits and considering giving up alcohol.

Be committed. You need to be 100% committed to stopping drinking as this is going to be challenging. You will be going against what has become society's norm and at the outset this could make you feel isolated and excluded. You are going to have to get used to a new kind of normal – one where you don't unwind, de-stress, celebrate, commiserate, relieve boredom, numb pain etc with a glass or ten of your favourite tipple.

Work out why you want to make this change and try to keep focused on the end goal.

Change your perception about alcohol. We are conditioned to accept that alcohol is a normal substance, It is in fact a powerful poison and a highly addictive drug. It is also the only drug you have to justify not taking. By changing the way you see alcohol, it is far easier to enjoy the process of quitting drinking.

Be positive. It is vital to keep positive to stop yourself falling back into drinking. Think about the language you are using. For example, I never once allowed myself to think or say out loud sentences like: "I'm going to try to stop drinking" or "I probably won't drink". I've unwaveringly stuck to assertive language like: "I'm going to stop drinking", "I'm not going to drink" and "I don't drink". Words matter and the words we choose can either lift us up or drag us down. Use positive language and make sure you are consistently looking forward to the positive outcomes of stopping drinking.

Be prepared. When you have been at the centre of drunken debauchery, you might find yourself coming up against resistance from your former drinking buddies and becoming vulnerable to peer pressure. You need to think about what you are going to tell people and how you are going to deflect the compulsion to drink. If you aren't properly armed, it is easy to fall back to your default position. I announced from the outset that I was stopping drinking for a year. Apart from the initial haranguing and general consternation, this worked well. It gave me a goal to work towards and it short cut the need for repeated conversations about why I wasn't drinking. I kept a fairly low profile during the first couple of months of getting sober to keep out of temptation's way. I discovered other ways to occupy myself such as yoga, hiking, reading, painting, singing and swimming. For the times when I was compelled to go out, then I always made sure I had an escape plan up my sleeve if things got tough.

Be realistic. Being sober doesn't wave a magic wand and make your problems disappear. At first, it is tough dealing with life without your good old trusty crutch, alcohol. You may also find that you are going to have to face up to some issues that you have suppressed for many years with alcohol. I know I did and my therapy involved a lot of reading about addiction and writing a blog to process my emotions. There are also some really supportive and completely non-judgemental closed Facebook groups such as Club Soda, One Year No Beer and Women Who Don't Drink, which I found helpful when I was struggling. The old adage goes: 'Good things come to those who wait'. Quitting drinking will deliver so much but don't expect everything to happen immediately. Have a little patience and over time you will reap the rewards.

Calling 'Time' on Drinking Culture

by LEIGH MATTHEWS

Although data on the prevalence of alcohol abuse amongst expats is limited, both anecdotal and clinical evidence suggest expats drink more frequently and excessively than their counterparts in their home countries. Roughly 24 out of every 219 (11%) of internationals who complete our initial questionnaire at Therapy in Barcelona select 'addiction' as a primary concern for which they require support. If you are an expat or aspiring to be one, it is critical to be aware of the expat vulnerability to imbibe excessively, especially if anyone tells you: *"You'll fit perfectly in to the expat partying lifestyle"* as Adrienne's cousins had prior to her move to Hong Kong.

Like the majority of expats, Adrienne had expected to slot seamlessly into life abroad but it is, as we see when expat life is stripped bare, a minefield of stressors. Numerous studies have shown stress in any population contributes to an increase in alcohol consumption. Culture shock, work pressures, dislocation from family and friends, homesickness, language barriers and isolation can all lead to challenges in expat adaptation. Substance abuse, including excess drinking, reflect the emotional toll expatriate life can incur and are by-products of expat attempts to cope and socialise. Add to that more liberal approaches to alcohol consumption in expat destinations and a higher prevalence of mental health issues in the expat population and, et voilà, you have your expat drinking problem. Paradoxically, excess alcohol consumption magnifies those mental health issues in the long run and individuals who come to the expat party with a family history of alcoholism are at a greater risk.

The ubiquity of booze in most cultures enables drinking problems to remain covert. Even when drinking is a staple of daily life, expats won't necessarily think of it in terms of problematic consumption. The stereotype of the rock bottom alcoholic veils the common white collar problem drinker. As with any population, expat willingness to disclose the problem of alcohol abuse is the first step to creating a culture of support in place of a culture of drinking. Ignorance, denial, shame and secrecy are all factors that perpetuate the problem.

The lure of alcohol and drugs as panaceas for the loneliness and the disruption of expat life is real. Prevention requires an 'eyes wide open' approach to expatriation. Seek information or therapy to develop a complete awareness of and develop healthy coping strategies for the shocks and stressors that come with the territory of expat life. Expatriate with intention. Choose alternative avenues for meeting people beyond bars: meetups, sports clubs, creative classes or book groups. Choose a different path to the 'work hard play hard' culture you may be tempted to succumb to. Learn strategies to disconnect and relax without alcohol. Select your network in your host country wisely: a sober crew is recommended. Preempt the possibility of getting trapped in booze culture by researching alternative paths before hitting your destination. Swap lychee martinis, *cervezas* or sake for sparkling water or non-alcoholic options. Mocktails can camouflage your self-preservation in the face of peer pressure. Choose better quality, expensive options and moderate consumption to appreciate the nuances of each drink. Commit to showing up for yourself, not for Happy Hour.

What you will find in an alcohol-free, or limited alcohol existence, living is just as Adrienne describes it: *"many dramatic changes, the most notable being that my mental health took a significant U-turn – my anxiety, anger and pessimism were replaced with contentment and positivity. My energy levels increased, I started sleeping really well, my face started to glow and I lost weight."*

If you suspect you might have an issue with alcohol, know that you are not alone. You don't need to hit rock bottom to seek help. Locate an expatriate therapy service of which there are plenty around, including online services. Look for AA meetings in your host country or join an AA Facebook Group. If you're not sure, try taking the AUDIT (Alcohol Use Disorders Identification Test) test to assess your relationship with alcohol.

Useful resources

The Sober Diaries by Clare Pooley

Kick the Drink... Easily! by Jason Vale

This Naked Mind: Control Alcohol by Annie Grace

The Unexpected Joy of being Sober by Catherine Gray

auditscreen.org (AUDIT test website)

Facebook groups: One Year No Beer, Club Soda, Women Who Don't Drink, Alcoholics Anonymous

CHAPTER
TWO

Exercise Caution
in Your Business Affairs

DEBORAH GRAY
BARCELONA (SPAIN)

Deborah Gray, 50
Canela HQ, Poble Nou, Barcelona

Photo by Maggie Michalowicz

Deborah Gray is the Managing Director of Canela, an award-winning public relations company with offices in Spain and Portugal. Originally from the UK, Deborah founded Canela in Barcelona in 2006 and, in defiance of the global recession, expanded operations to Madrid in 2008 and to Lisbon in 2010. She leads a team of over twenty communications consultants who manage PR campaigns for the European Commission, Dyson, Sony and other household names. In 2019, Canela was awarded the honour of the Best PR Agency in Spain and in June 2020 was ranked as the 4th Best PR Agency to Work for in Europe. She lives in the countryside near Barcelona with her partner and their two Anglo-Franco-Catalan children.

Exercise Caution
in Your Business Affairs

I came to Spain, for a year at the age of 29, having made decent progress in my career in public relations in London. I was on a good wage and had a mortgage on a flat. I was confident that a year away from it all would do me no harm and that I could return and pick up my career where I left off. I had just lived through the dot.com boom which had left me feeling work weary; I remember thinking "There must be more to life than this!". My idea was to take some time out, teach English, learn a language, and have my 'Eat Pray Love' year in the sun. I moved to Tarragona in Catalonia knowing no-one, I couldn't speak the language, neither Spanish or Catalan, and I had never been a teacher before. It seems utterly crazy looking back and with hindsight, I was probably experiencing an early midlife crisis.

During my first year of teaching, I went skiing with friends and broke my anterior cruciate ligament; I had to spend three months away from the classroom with my leg elevated. I basically lost the months between Christmas and Easter. So, when it came the end of the school year, I felt cheated out of the experience I had hoped to have and opted to stay for one more year. Just one.

After a year in Tarragona I decided to move to Barcelona to experience life in a big city. A love interest appeared on the scene, and after a second year of living here, my Spanish became fluent enough to explore alternative ways of earning a living. I began to consider the possibility of getting a job doing what I knew best: public relations. The first obstacle I had to overcome was a common frame of reference. When I told people that I was looking for a job in public relations, they understood it to mean handing out fliers for discos and clubs (which is what 'public relations' means directly translated into Spanish).

I suppose it takes a certain kind of naiveté or optimism to assume that you can enter the job market in a country where you didn't grow up, whose language you barely dominate, in a sector which relies so heavily on cultural insights. It soon became all too clear that the career I had been building in the UK counted for absolutely nothing in Spain. Finding work meant having to start over again from scratch. I didn't have the network, the knowledge, the contacts nor the cultural references. I found myself being offered unpaid internships. I was, as the Spanish say, *'entre la espada y la pared'* (caught between the sword and the wall).

I went to see a headhunter who put it to me straight, "You will never make it here. You don't have the contacts. The only way you will succeed is if you set up your own business."

But one thing is for sure, you can't start a PR agency without a client.

I held that thought and despite all the odds was eventually offered a job at a Spanish PR agency. I was there for a year before they sacked me. The company was run by two women who had an entirely different approach to public relations than mine. We were obliged to sign in and out as we arrived and left the office as if we were factory workers. I refused to do it. Public relations is a creative, ideas-based business which requires brainstorming and constant communication, but there was such a climate of fear in that agency that people barely spoke to each other. One of the bosses repeatedly picked on the team members, so employees came in and out like a revolving door. The better my relationships became with clients and team members the more the unpleasantness increased. After one particular incident, I wrote an email to the big boss saying "You have a responsibility as a General Manager and as a human being to put an end to the bullying that goes on in this workplace".

By 6pm the same day I had my *'finiquito'* (P45) in my hand.

I had one client at this agency with whom I got on very well. Not surprisingly, he was shocked at my overnight departure and got in contact with me to ask what had happened. He told me, "If you set up your own agency, I will come with you." It was my 'now or never' moment. So, I took the plunge and made the decision to set up my own PR agency. I called it Canela because *canela* is the Spanish word for cinnamon which is used to flavour Mediterranean dishes and it is also easy to pronounce in all languages and, in my startup phase euphoria, I had a plan for global domination. There is also an expression in Spanish, which means if something is *'canela en rama'* (a stick of canela) it is high quality. Most importantly of all, the domain name was available. That first client remained my client for the next 10 years.

The first year of setting up Canela was absolutely amazing. I loved every single minute of it. I was on a permanent high. It was like the hormone surge you get after giving birth but a year's supply. There was so much to celebrate during that first year: the first client, the design of the logo, the website going live, the first invoice being paid, the second client, the first freelancer, the first employee, the first office, the second invoice being paid. It felt like all my stars had aligned and I was finally on the right path.

Setting up the agency also coincided with me ending my relationship with the aforementioned 'love interest'. Occasionally the universe just sends you a sign that it is time to shake it all up and get rid of the things that are holding you back. I could see that this man did not respect what I was trying to achieve. His lack of interest in my business was the final nail in the relationship's coffin which is ironic if you consider that my motive for going back into PR was so that I could stay in Spain with him.

By the end of the first year we had four clients, a shared office in El Borne, one full-time employee, one intern and two freelancers, and I had a new love interest. By the end of the second year it became obvious that we needed to open an office in Madrid if we were to compete with other PR agencies for major accounts. I knew the time had come to contract someone senior, i.e. someone expensive.

I placed a job advertisement and got a shortlist of two people, both of whom I interviewed in the café at Atocha train station in Madrid. As a rule of thumb when hiring, I always conduct half the interview in Spanish and half the interview in English. The interview was going well until we switched to English and the interviewee, despite having put on his CV that he spoke English fluently, was unable to express himself in English. Not one word. I now make it a rule to conduct a short telephone interview with everyone before scheduling any kind of face-to-face interview.

Luckily, the second interviewee could do everything she claimed to be able to do on her CV, and she became the Director of Canela in Madrid. The next step to Canela's world domination was underway. In my personal life, my love interest had morphed into someone I knew I wanted to spend the rest of my life with and we started talking about having children. No sooner had I hired the senior person to open our office in Madrid, than I became pregnant. And as soon as I was pregnant, the global recession set in. After two years of plenty, came five years of famine.

As with the more recent Coronavirus in 2020, the effects of the global recession in 2008 were felt especially hard in Spain. The economy basically crumbled. Most of our existing clients cut their budgets or stopped investing in PR altogether. The market seemed to stagnate for years, during which time my two children were born. On returning to work from my first maternity leave, the first thing I had to do was let two of my team members go, one of whom had been with Canela right from the beginning. This person had walked from one side of Barcelona to the other with me to buy our first computer. He had driven me in his own car to IKEA to buy the furniture for our first office. Telling this person that there was no longer a job for him at Canela was one of the hardest conversations I have ever had.

The other challenges I now faced had far less to do with being a foreigner and much more to do with being the female parent. I don't like to use the expression 'working Mum' for two reasons: 1. It's so loaded as its 'stay at home' counterpart 2. I believe putting the word 'working' before 'Mum' is like putting the word 'two' before 'twins'.

I now, like every other parent who has a job they are passionate about, had to find the balance between continuing to be the kind of professional I wanted to be and becoming the kind of parent I wanted to be. I took Miriam Stoppard's advice: "The best childcare solution is the one that works for you.". My childcare solution was a 'hard finish' time for myself three days a week so I could be at the school gates and employ a canguru (babysitter) for the other two days.

With a leaner team we ploughed on, and by 2013 Spain began limping its way back to an economic recovery. New business requests started pouring in. We won a whole host of new clients including some major household names. To service these new clients we hired new team members, both senior and junior. The number of employees in Madrid overtook the number of employees in Barcelona. We expanded to bigger offices in Madrid and moved to an office on the Passeig de Gràcia in Barcelona. Clients often asked us about doing their PR for them in Portugal. It occurred to me that I was missing a trick. I began to put out feelers for someone to set up a Canela office in Portugal. We found a suitable person and opened an office in Lisbon. We went from being a Spanish agency to being an Iberian agency with a foothold in both countries and offices in three cities. Our billing jumped from €750,000 in 2014 to €2.400,000 in 2015. We kept our billing levels at over €2 million for the next four years.

Having three different offices does mean that I need to travel to see the team, take part in new business pitches and attend client events with the press. I generally go once a month to Madrid and once a quarter to Lisbon and stay overnight. These trips are 'negotiated' long in advance with my partner to make sure he is there to cover the school pick up and drop offs. Those nights away from my family in a hotel are an absolute luxury. I enjoy a long bath, read a book, get to finish a thought process, and can 'lie in' in the morning.

Would I be a better parent if I wasn't running a PR agency? It depends on how you define what being a good parent is. I am away from home for at least one, sometimes two nights a month. On those occasions, their dad puts them in pre-school care in the mornings and they love to moan about it. I get tired and stressed when there's a big pitch or we lose a major client. At the same time both my daughter and my son get to see first-hand what it is like to run a business. They like to get involved with ideas for PR campaigns and they love visiting the office and wheeling round on the office chairs, using the coffee machine, stealing the stationery and any leftover client goodies. I am providing an example to my daughter and perhaps even more importantly to my son that a parent can be successful in their chosen career and still be there at the school gate with a hug and packet of biscuits.

Once our billing went over the €2 million threshold we started to receive nominations for 'Agency of the Year' and 'Best Agency to Work for'. Our campaigns were given awards in both Spain and Portugal as well as internationally. In 2019 we received a call to say we had been chosen as the Best PR Agency in Spain. I was invited to Madrid to receive the award, and I had my 'Olivia Colman Oscars moment' on the podium alongside famous TV personalities and the Mayor of Madrid. My speech was in Spanish and the audience were forgiving when I struggled to get my words out. I did it. I went from being offered unpaid internships to receiving the prize for the best PR agency in Spain. I wish my Dad could have seen it happen; I know how proud he would have been.

I picked up the prize in November 2019. By January 2020 there was talk of a virus in China. In March 2020 our income dropped by 50% overnight. I had half the income and all the team members, and all the offices to pay rent on. It was like 2008 all over again. Only this time I didn't have the option to let people go during a face-to-face meeting; I was forced to do it over Skype. And on it goes.

Of the 'then again too few to mention' regrets I have, the most notable one is it would have been nice to enjoy a real maternity leave where I could have disconnected entirely from the worries of owning a business. The Spanish system allows for only sixteen weeks paid leave, but even if the allocation had been longer, I am not sure I would have been able to benefit from it. Owning a business is quite simply relentless; you never get to switch off. Also, if I am completely honest with myself, scrolling through work emails on my smartphone while breastfeeding probably helped save my sanity during those moments of bovine despair.

It's actually quite hard to give advice to anyone in business without sounding like a Richard Branson post on LinkedIn. Basically, any wisdom I have to offer was written down one hundred years ago by Max Ehrmann in "Desiderata" which I have pinned up on my fridge and has been my mantra since I discovered it in my late 20s. *"Exercise caution in your business affairs, for the world is full of trickery. But let this not blind you to what virtue there is; many persons strive for high ideals, and everywhere life is full of heroism."*

I have also learned that I am pretty much unemployable.

Exercise Caution
in Your Business Affairs

by DEBORAH GRAY

Setting up a business in a country where you didn't grow up requires a certain kind of optimism that borders on blind faith. You need a really heavy layer of thick skin and the ability to bounce back from anything that life throws at you. You will have no time for self-doubt and must have a best foot forward mentality. The good news is, if you've moved abroad you probably have all those qualities anyway. I can't speak for every circumstance but here are some lessons learned which I hope may be useful for others.

Don't define yourself exclusively by what you do for a living because it can all disappear overnight through no fault of your own. I have been a business owner through the global recession of 2008 and the Covid-19 pandemic and on both occasions I could see my business crumbling away in front of my very own eyes. At times like these, it is essential to have other interests because they will help keep everything in perspective and keep you sane. Be proud of your professional achievements and rightly so, but make sure that they are not the only story you have to tell. Run triathlons, have an allotment, join a choir, volunteer, whatever floats your boat – just don't put all your eggs in one basket.

Don't take yourself too seriously. As a non-native you will inevitably make cultural and language gaffs. When I make a Spanish language mistake in front of my team I refer to it as my *encanto guiri* (foreigner's charm). I sent a company-wide email asking the team to make a special effort to terrorise (*aterrorizar*) new employees when I had meant to ask to help them settle in (*aterrizar*). On occasions like these, the only choice is to have good laugh at yourself. Own your gaffs and don't be embarrassed by them. Make it work in your favour. At the end of the day most of us are suckers for a foreign accent.

Make sure you choose your partner very, very carefully. Especially if you want to have children. I would fully advocate a pre-nuptial agreement, not for the division of wealth in the event of divorce, but for the division of labour in the event of having children. Do not let the other parent bring the "I earn most therefore my career takes precedence over yours" argument to the table. Carving out any kind of satisfactory career in a country where you didn't grow up is an absolute miracle, so don't be bullied into abandoning it when children come along. Given that – in most cases – you will not have an extended family network around you for support, your partner's willingness and ability to do their fair share will be an essential part of you being able to continue along your chosen path. Make some serious boundaries about what is possible and what is not possible in terms of commitments and family logistics. Strive hard for that dark-coloured, oddly-shaped part in the middle of the Venn Diagram that unites the kind of professional you want to be with the kind of parent you want to be and the kind of partner you want to be with the kind of person you want to be. It is all possible – it just requires a lot of compromises on everyone's part not just yours.

Know yourself very well, especially your weak points. Make sure that the team you build around you are complementary to you. There will be things that you simply can't do because you don't have the knowledge or the experience – and it doesn't matter. Don't be tempted to micro-manage just to have a sense of control. In the wise words of Elsa in 'Frozen' film you need to "let it go". Bring your unique added value to the table and let other people bring theirs.

Trust your own instincts and act on them. As an expat, it stands to reason that you will be a risk-taker by nature. If you've got this far you must be doing something right! Be sure to listen to all the advice you are given, especially from those who have different points of view and experiences from yours. But the most important thing is to be at peace with the decisions you have taken. Own your mistakes. You're going to make quite a few but in the long term they won't matter. Let your team make mistakes so they can learn from them too. Be kind and be forgiving. In my experience most people are always doing their best.

Don't expect to get rich. If you want to get rich stay in your own country and climb the ladder there. Nobody sets up a business in Spain in the hope of becoming rich. You need another motive like wanting to build your life here, because you have fallen in love with the climate, the food, the wine or somebody. A quick Google search reveals that the UK occupies the eighth position in the ranking of easiest countries to run a business. Spain doesn't even make the Top 20. Be clear and stay clear about the motives you have for doing what you're doing.

WHAT THE EXPERT SAYS

Exercise Caution
in Your Business Affairs

by LEIGH MATTHEWS

Whether you are lured to expat life for love, adventure or some other fancy, you will need to get down to business at some point in your journey. Working life, including job and career opportunities, work-life balance and job security should be, though often are not, paramount considerations when choosing the right location. Countries' rankings on these factors vary wildly according to the Internations Urban Work Life Index 2020. One of the most resonant counsels from expats is: "find a portable career."

If you don't have a portable career, moving to a new country can feel limiting, especially when language barriers exist. However, for the most successful of globally mobile individuals, including spouses accompanying their partners on expat assignments, a new destination offers opportunities for career reinvention. Teaching, consulting, blogging, freelance writing, virtual assistance, translating, graphic design, web design, social media management, crafts, photography – many opportunities exist for upskilling or generalising skills from your passport country career to your expat career. The Covid-19 pandemic, global restrictions on movement and increased work from home culture has forced many individuals and businesses to 'pivot' but pivoting has been as integral to many expats' lives as luggage.

Expatriate entrepreneurs or "expat-preneurs" are a phenomenon and logically rise out of their growth mindset. This mindset drives expats, fuelling them with the desire to stretch and persist, embrace failures as growth and challenges as opportunities. Expats are ideal entrepreneurs with a stomach for discomfort, uncertainty and exposure to novel ideas across cultures, including those not tested in all countries. Some will be alert to business opportunities and gaps in the market and some, like Deborah Gray, will launch a venture in their new country from a solid educational background and professional experience. An Internations survey* found that one in seven self-employed expats moved abroad to work as a regular employee and decided to run their own business further down the road. Business services and consulting, primarily in healthcare, lead the way, followed by the retail and wholesale sector, food and tourism sectors, education and research industries and legal services.

The expat-preneur path will add some degree of challenge to the already complex expat journey, with business-related bureaucracy, visa, work permit, academic recognition and tax hassles to be tackled. Thorough research and preparation will be essential. Striking a balance between gung-ho ambition and considered risk is the middle way of the expat-preneurs who make it.

Deborah's advice couldn't be better: find identity beyond the bounds of career since economic upheavals

*Expat Entrepreneurs around the world 2016

and the whims of the market can swiftly upend your business. Be prepared for humbling errors if you are managing a business as a non-native with language barriers to boot. You will make mistakes! Find mentors. Follow the trailblazers. Go with your instincts and have a strong measure of judgement. Carefully curate an exceptional team and partner with someone who can share the load. Exercise humility, curiosity and, most importantly, embrace your unemployability as an opportunity to reinvent yourself and prepare to be surprised as you forge a new path.

Useful resources

expatica.com/es/working/self-employment/starting-a-business-in-spain (advice on legal framework)

emprenedoria.barcelonactiva.cat/emprenedoria/en/emprenedoria/library-of-the-entrepreneur/index.jsp (resources available to entrepreneurs in Barcelona)

startupgrind.com/barcelona (A networking group for entrepreneurs)

CHAPTER
THREE

Married Plus Four,
a Trail Between Four Countries

AVIVIT DELGOSHEN
LONDON (UK)

Avivit Delgoshen, 42
At home, Sutton, London

Photo by Luke Baker

When she manages to carve out time from being a full-on mum, Avivit Delgoshen is a TV news producer, an amateur photographer, a choir singer, a cake baker and an aspiring gardener. She studied international relations at the Hebrew University of Jerusalem and has worked for global media organisations in Israel and the UK. Her eclectic musical taste links her heritage in the Middle East with her years living in European capitals. Together with her husband and four kids they are settling down in south London, the latest but not the final stop in a journey to discover the oddities of raising a bicultural family in a multicultural world.

Married Plus Four,
a Trail Between Four Countries

It was on a flight from Tel Aviv to Paris that it started to make sense. My then eight-year-old daughter was sitting just across the aisle from me, next to an Israeli mother and her daughter, chatting away to them in Hebrew. When the air stewardess came to offer drinks, she answered immediately in English, and helped her neighbours with their orders.

"So how come you speak English so well?" they asked in Hebrew.

"My dad is English," she replied.

Thinking they'd got the full picture of my daughter's upbringing, the conversation continued.

"So, will you be going to Euro Disney on your holiday in France?" the woman asked.

"Oh, no, we live in France," my daughter replied.

"Ah. So, do you also speak French?"

"Yes, since I was little. I grew up in Belgium."

At this point the lady and her daughter looked at each other and then at me, bewildered.

My daughter explained: "I was born in England but shortly after we moved to Belgium, and then we moved to Israel, and now we live in Paris."

Simple!

Overhearing her laying out her life story in such a concise, matter-of-fact way was a relief. I realised that everything we'd managed to pack into her eight years of life as part of an expat family – moving to four countries, speaking three languages, switching in and out six houses and still not having a place to call "home" – had not caused confusion or muddled her identity. She sounded like a young citizen of the world, with a family travelling alongside her.

By contrast, the first time I moved to a new country I was nearly 30. I'd fallen in love with an Englishman, a journalist I'd met working in Jerusalem. It was a real-life case of love at first sight, but until we met it hadn't crossed my mind that I would date someone who wasn't Jewish, let alone some bloke from another corner of the world. It seemed inconceivable that the daughter of Iranian Kurdish Jewish parents living in Israel would end up with some English guy born-and-raised in the West Country to one-hundred-percent British parents. Clearly fate had other plans.

When we decided to give our relationship a serious go – which included agreeing to actually live in the same country – I packed up a big red suitcase with my favourite CDs, a Hebrew-English dictionary and some warm clothes, and flew to London, launching on a journey with absolutely no idea where it would lead.

We've now been together for 14 years, have four kids who were born in three different countries, and a puppy we're still trying to train. In quiet moments, we often find ourselves trying to figure out how this vibrant, chaotic, multi-cultural family came into being, and how it has survived more than a decade of expat living.

The first twist in the plot came barely a year into our working life in London. We were a newly married couple, living in a sweet but tiny apartment near Tower Bridge. I was three months pregnant and it was time for a scan.

"This is your first scan, right?" said the eager young sonographer, her face glowing in the dark x-ray room of St Thomas's hospital. "So, you don't know you have twins, right? And they're identical!"

I saw my husband's face turn completely white. I burst into uncontrolled laughter. Nothing had prepared us for this. We'd gone from a care-free pair scootering around London to the soon-to-be parents of twins in a flash of a second. Our apartment was barely big enough for the both of us, let alone two more. Joy and fear mixed. I felt almost guilty for feeling anxious, when it was clearly a moment to be thrilled. How are we all going to fit in the flat? How can I breastfeed two at once? Just how big am I going to get? And how am I going to handle twins without my family and friends on hand?

While waddling from one check-up to another with what felt like a summer-sale load of watermelons in my tummy, my husband found a way of complicating things even further.

"I've been offered a job in Brussels," he announced one evening. His company was sending him to be the deputy bureau chief in the EU capital, with the start date pencilled in for a few weeks before the twins were due. It meant that most of my ninth month of pregnancy would be spent alone in London while he was in Brussels. That didn't pass muster with our parents, who immediately lined up to help, mine planning to fly in from Israel and his to take the train from Bath. It was all hands on deck to try to stick to a schedule that would involve moving country, house and job in a matter of weeks, while taking care of the small issue of giving birth to twin girls in one city and moving them to another barely a month later. My husband often mumbles about most divorces being caused by moving country, house or job, or by the arrival of kids. We were attempting all four at once.

The first couple of weeks after the delivery were a hormonal rollercoaster. My heart was crying for the people I loved and missed so much in Israel, who were unable to share in the joy of the new arrivals or comfort me in those moments of agony and despair. My husband divided his time between London and Brussels, shuttling back at the weekends on the Eurostar to try to help, juggling work with the demands of the babies as best he could after I'd exhausted every drip of energy dealing with the sleepless nights during the week. Hanging over it all was the impending move to another country. It could have been a near-perfect recipe for a breakup. We were too tired to even argue about it.

Barely five weeks after the girls were born we were on a train under the Channel, staying at first in a temporary apartment in Brussels. With very little knowledge of anything Belgium-related, apart from chocolate and waffles and the weirdly popular Mannequin Pis (pissing boy) statue, we arrived in Brussels with essentially only the address for our future home in a culturally diverse corner of the city. We waited several days for the truck carrying our household goods to arrive. The day we got the keys we walked the girls to the building in their new double pushchair. As we entered, knowing we were on the fourth floor, we were pleased to discover a smart new elevator. But to our dismay it wasn't big enough for the two of us, let alone our ridiculously expensive, supposedly fantastic double buggy. Up the stairs we climbed, armed with the babies and all their accoutrements, my husband feeling the daggers from my eyes in his back, appreciating the sunlight streaming through the large double-glazed windows but not much else.

The tiny lift, clearly overlooked in my husband's otherwise detailed apartment search, turned into a first lesson in resourcefulness – if you have to start each day carting two babies down four flights of stairs in the freezing cold (it was December) before getting anything done, everything else feels pretty straightforward. It was also a lesson in surviving as an expat: there is only so much you can plan for when you move to a new place. The one thing you don't plan for will almost inevitably end up being the biggest irritation – if you let it be. Sometimes it's best to just suck it up and roll with it.

It was time for the babies' first vaccination and that meant registering with the Belgian health services. Getting through the bureaucratic hurdles of settling into a new country is hard enough as it is but doing it in a language you hardly speak is doubly challenging. Brussels is the European Union's mothership and a melting pot for dozens of African and Middle Eastern countries, but despite it being such a cosmopolitan city, we were surprised that local officials and many shops basically refused to speak English. Every encounter was a head-to-head battle. I say "Bonjour", they say "Bonjour". I ask "Parlez-vous anglais?", they say "Non" and that's it. Cold stares. You're expected to speak fluent French or be ignored.

The European debt crisis, which struck in late 2009 and was still making headlines four years later, meant my husband was not at home nearly as much as I had hoped. A brutal first winter – not easy for an Israeli raised on the Mediterranean – meant that almost every trip outside involved a confrontation with driving rain, sleet or snow, with two babies in tow. Days went by without speaking to anyone. Social interactions were reduced to encounters with our neighbours in the building – a Swedish couple with a classically blue-eyed, blond young boy and a Majorcan couple with a fiery little girl. We became a valuable support group, sharing information, comparing notes and cheering each other's spirits as we went along.

Around the time our girls turned one it was time to find them a nursery. They had only just shown signs of understanding my Hebrew and my husband's English, and now, to complicate things further, we had to choose which third language to add – French or Flemish. There is a lot of research into the benefits of exposing kids to different languages from an early age. But the question is how best to do it. Should we both speak to them in our native tongue and let them deal with the nursery language separately? Should we address them in the language they seem to understand best? Should we mix up words from all three and strengthen what they already know? And when they develop a debilitating stutter in multiple languages, do we give them a pat on the back or stop speaking to them all together?

We chose a local French-speaking creche overseen by a fearsome Moroccan-Belgian woman, whose own mother toiled in the kitchen making cous-cous for the kids. Leaving the girls in the hands of strangers with whom I couldn't really communicate had me thinking of creative ways of bridging the language gap. I mastered the nursery terminology in no time – translating each day from the notebook the creche used to communicate with parents about what their children had eaten, how long they had slept or whether they pooped. I learnt French nursery songs to sing for the girls, watching them daily on YouTube. I picked up a bizarrely eclectic range of vocabulary. To this day I know all about spiders knitting boots, fingers dancing, animal tails dunked in oil and elephants bouncing.

By the time they were three we could safely say that the girls were trilingual. The French kicked in while Hebrew and English were going strong. When they started to correct my French pronunciation ("Mommy it's *Maman*, not *Mama*") – I knew they were fine. While they were able to communicate in three languages, even I managed to grow beyond nursery rhymes and extend my ability to hold a conversation, or at least fake it better.

Once the girls were settled it was time for me to get back out there, find a job and start exercising my brain again. It left me with a difficult choice – should I focus on something professional but have my daughters spend long days in childcare, or give up my professional career and find work that would allow me to continue to be an anchor for my family?

I chose the latter and still, to this day, have no regrets. While my husband continued to progress in his career, I was having to reinvent myself everywhere we went. When searching for a job it was not about what I wanted to do, but what I could do in the constraints we had as expats – the jobs that were available, language difficulties, not having a support network for after-school care, not knowing how long we would be staying around. My work choices have produced some random outcomes: I've taught Hebrew in French to Belgian school children; edited video for an international charity; done public relations for a university. But it's all been instructive in some way, even if it felt like a regression in others. That said, it made one thing clear – my life advice to my kids is: if you plan to move countries a lot in the future, pick a transferable profession.

Starting off a family with twins is exhausting, but that meant the arrival of our third daughter felt like a stroll in the park. Although I ended up having another last-minute Caesarean operation, the Belgian postnatal care was exceptional. They are big believers in kinesitherapy, which focuses on the rehabilitation of the body after childbirth and is widely practiced.

But the luxury of raising a new baby in a familiar place was not one we were spoiled with. As we got comfortable in Belgium after nearly five years, it was time to think about our next move. My husband's contract was about to end and a new assignment was due. As ever, where to and when was decided at the last minute. Yet this time there was some upside to starting anew – he was being sent to Jerusalem, effectively a trip home for me.

The Middle Eastern sun welcomed us as we landed in Tel Aviv on a blisteringly hot August day. The taxi drove us up the hills into Jerusalem. It was rush hour on a Friday evening – the time that marks the beginning of Shabbat, the sabbath. From the taxi we could see men, women and children in dark clothing running to make their last journey before the sunset call for 24 hours of rest. As a crowd of Hassidic Jews crossed the road in front of us at a traffic light, my daughter turned to me and asked, "Why are these people all dressed like that?"

I knew Jerusalem was going to provoke a lot of questions.

We arrived during the Israel-Gaza war of 2014, when Israeli forces were fighting back against waves of rocket fire from Palestinian militants in the Gaza Strip. Since I'd left Israel, the militants' rockets had grown more effective and were now reaching almost to Jerusalem, 90 kilometres from Gaza. On our first night in our new home we were welcomed by the sound of sirens warning of a missile attack. We faced a hideous dilemma – should we wake the children in the middle of the night and rush to a shelter, probably traumatising them; or was it likely a false alarm and we should let them go on sleeping soundly.

We purposefully hadn't told the girls much about the fighting before arriving, believing that ignorance was probably the best protection. But that first night was a serious reality check and took much of the joy out of being back home. It reminded me that despite all my love for the place I'm from, it is troubled and faces very real threats that can leave children sleeping in air-raid shelters. Suddenly I missed the sanity of living in Europe.

Returning to Israel after seven years abroad was a chance to bring my children closer to my upbringing and introduce my husband to parts of my life and culture he wasn't familiar with. But it also meant that my husband had free rein to be the complaining outsider and I was the one on the receiving end. "Why are they driving like maniacs?", "How can people survive here, it's insanely expensive!", "Why does every conversation in Hebrew sound like an argument?", "Why is there so much rubbish on the beaches?" All the while I was trying to make our life in Israel as hassle-free as possible, dealing with the dreaded energy and telephone companies, managing our girls' school, nursery and after-school activities, organising meetings with friends and family, hoping maybe – just maybe – we would stay longer than the usual three to five years of an international journalist's assignment. Maybe much longer.

Early spring is normally when we begin to discuss our next move – about enough time to end up in the new country before the school year begins in September. It became like a ticking biological clock. When nature renews itself, we also tend to seek renewal ourselves, and if an opportunity to move to an interesting new destination is on the table, we usually toy with the idea, sometimes for fun, sometimes for a real chance to start afresh. But this time it was different. It was a conversation I did not want to have. I did not want to leave Israel. At least not yet.

With each move, the emotional toll was growing. Setting up a life in a new place is never smooth sailing. It takes at least a year to get the basics covered, whether schools, grocery shops or finding the most reliable doctors, dentists, swimming teachers and handymen. The second year is usually a chance to bed down new friendships, and by the third year, just as you start to feel comfortable and are enjoying life, you have to start thinking about the next move.

So it proved with Jerusalem. Just as we were getting truly settled in – even planting a kumquat tree alongside the lemons and olives in the garden of our gorgeous house – a new job opportunity came up for my husband: a chance to move to France and run the bureau in The City of Lights.

I discovered I was pregnant with our fourth child around the same time. It took us by surprise but nonetheless, we quickly adjusted to the new reality and I had to surrender my hope of giving birth in Israel. I was mentally preparing to leave my home country for the second time, battling doubts and fears about whether we were doing the right thing. But knowing that doubt is the biggest enemy, especially when explaining to children that the world as they know it is about to change, I kept thinking about what we promised each other in our marriage ceremony: to build roots and wings, to know deeply where we are from and what we are about so we can leave the nest and explore, knowing we will always have a place to come back to.

Telling the girls about our decision involved a long session of tears, mostly on my part. I tried to reassure them that striking out on a new adventure didn't mean giving up on what we had – they should instead see it as an opportunity to try something different. I don't know where I found the strength to pull this conversation through but I even managed to convince myself.

With a new destination on the map and another baby on its way, we set out for Paris. As usual, it was a last-minute contract agreement, which meant we had to move in haste. I was seven months pregnant, hadn't seen the school the girls were signed up for, didn't have a hospital to give birth in, didn't even have an address to move into. We were warned that managing to find an apartment to rent in Paris during August was about as likely as finding no queue at the Eiffel Tower. But hey, we'd sort it out. We had become experts at packing up and leaving to the unknown, and this time was no different.

Our temporary apartment was bizarrely on Avenue Montaigne, one of the swankiest streets in the city, just off the Champs-Élysées, packed with boutiques, designer stores and pink Lamborghinis racing up and down at night. We stayed above a Chanel workshop, looking out on the Plaza Athénée hotel, the discreet hideaway of models and movie stars. There wasn't a restaurant or grocery store within 500 metres that didn't cost an arm and a leg. A pregnant mother with three children in tow was completely alien to the neighbourhood. From that first impression, Paris looked attractive but felt somewhat unattainable.

The pinnacle of irritation was French bureaucracy. It is a specialised form of torture and it applies everywhere: from renting a flat to registering for public transport cards; from issuing a residence document to ordering photo prints. Everything felt like an uphill struggle aimed at pushing us away, too much of a pain for the French to deal with. There is a moment in every meeting with French officialdom where the lips of the person you're dealing with tighten and you know the next words out of their mouths are going to be: *"Non, c'est pas possible."*

After a few weeks and nearly ready to pop, we moved into an apartment that was miraculously big enough to fit our expanding family. Its distance from the school meant we had to use public transport for our daily school-run with three kids and a baby, part of our attempt to go a little more green. What we didn't realise was that not all metro stations have escalators to carry a pushchair and changing buses in rush hour is impossible: the buses are packed and sometimes they'd only allow one or two of us on.

Finding an Uber Max to carry our group of five is a rare chance, and driving through Paris is a suicide mission. Every time I tried to drive I was on edge, and in any case the car had to be parked in a garage miles from the apartment, four levels below ground. So we stuck to the original plan and transformed from having two cars and three kids in Israel to four kids and effectively no car in Paris.

It was those mundane annoyances that tainted the Parisian picture-perfect image I had in mind. Our expat stint in the city lasted only two years but long enough to realise that when the cumulative toll turns greater than the enjoyment of living in a new place, it's harder to justify to yourself and to your children all the compromises you have had to make in order to move your life there. It might be that if we had been living in Paris in a different time, in a different stage of our lives and had to worry only about ourselves, we would have enjoyed it so much more. But raising children in the city, where six months of the year you can't walk on the grass in its parks, where you passively inhale at least two cigarettes every time you take the trip to school, where every encounter with French authorities is like broken record of 'non', is a tall order.

Our two-year adventure in Paris is now a distant memory, but it was an important lesson in how much we are willing to adapt to life in new places as a family and as expats. In time, we'll no doubt jump on the opportunity to visit Paris for a long weekend of dining out and breathing in the beauty of this city and reminiscing about parenthood and expathood, with or without the kids. But for now, we are back in London, settling down into a place we're making our 'home'.

In an odd way, expat life prepared us for the social distancing that so many have been struggling to live with. We just had to default to life as expats – being away from family and friends, communicating with grandparents via video chat, planning our next get together long in advance, even if it means waiting for months. The flexibility and adjustability needed in times of change have been our family staple for the last decade. I can't say for certain if we are here to stay or is it merely a rest stop on a prolonged expat journey. But for now, we promised ourselves that we will not talk about moving on. We will give ourselves time to grow some roots and let nature take its course.

REFLECTIONS

Married Plus Four,
a Trail Between Four Countries

by AVIVIT DELGOSHEN

They say it takes a village to raise a child. But when you're an expat you're giving up on your familiar support network and you need to build your own village from scratch everywhere you go, in unexpected and unfamiliar environment, sometimes in a language you don't even speak.

Cry it out, laugh it off. Life in a foreign country will inevitably bring about moments of painful absurdity, and those could result in either banging your head against the wall and wishing to be on the first plane out, or by shrugging them off and curating them into a collection of entertaining stories to tell. Almost every encounter in a language I did not dominate had put me in a lesser position, often without the courage or the ability to answer back, to question or to demand some reasonable explanation. Allow the blood rush to wash over you, cry it all out and let those frustrations be heard by your partner or a friend, because soon you will look back at those encounters and you'll find those irritations turning into amusing anecdotes that your children would love to hear over and over again.

Tune in, tune out. While the excitement of new sights and sounds and the prospects of discovery and adventure are the thrill that gets us globetrotters going, it is having children that turns this choice of lifestyle into a recipe for loneliness and seclusion. Making a life in a new country means leaving your natural habitat where cultural norms and social connections are mostly to be taken for granted. With the birth of my first-born twin girls, the absence of my family and friends was what shook me to understand that from now on it is our little family cell that would need to thrive on its own without the casual or immediate support from the people who are no longer close by, and without the social influences that would inevitably funnel our way forward in life. But being away from our homelands has been an opportunity to tune in, to focus on our family's make up, to strengthen the bonds and shape our own original character as a cross-cultural family. The expat family will now be your expanded family abroad. You are not the only one dealing with the emotional and practical aspects of raising children in foreign countries, so reach out, make connections, share and exchange experiences. You're not alone.

Living everywhere, coming from nowhere. If you'd ask my kids where they are from, they would not be able to give you a straight simple answer. To put it simply, their roots are not in a place that they can name but rather in our family as a collective being. Wherever this family is, this is where "home" is. I had to accept that the childhood I have designed for my children is very different to the way I was brought up. My upbringing and that of my children follow complete opposite trajectories – while I was born with very strong roots in the place I'm from and later on in life spanned out to the world and have been forming my identity in relation to the various places we've lived in, my children have been born into this nomad existence and, as they grow more mature and are aware they are forming their own sense of identity, as citizens of the world. I was relieved to learn that my children do have a "name" – they are TCKs, Third Culture Kids, children who spend most of their developing years in countries that are not their parents' homeland. And learning the ropes of parenting TCKs probably needs a definition in itself.

Appreciate the new, celebrate the old. Living in a foreign country comes with an open invitation to adopt something new of the sounds, tastes and aesthetics of the place. Whether it's French music playing in the kitchen, the odd Belgian chocolate box ordered on special occasions or the dishes and rugs from the Middle East, our house is a reflection of the cultural influences we've had. We've welcomed new traditions into our family, but the stronger elements that have become our family traditions are those we've been carrying with us since we can remember, those we bring from our home. I found that the natural process of blending in, assimilating into the country you temporarily call home also pulls you deeper into your roots and the cultural thread that continues to weave within you. And it's important to make the effort to celebrate the old traditions and persist in it wherever you are in the world, because they are the ones that will hold and become a part of the cultural thread that weaves through your children as well.

Zoom in, zoom out. It is very easy to lose yourself in a new country and focus on the day-to-day chores, challenges and cheers that keep you forever stimulated. You want to learn the language, to make friends, to find childcare, to get your children settled in schools and after-school activities, to plan weekend excursions and trips in the country and so much more of the mundane activities that seem to never end… and of course to find time to breathe, reflect and take it all in. When you're an expat you're too busy to think about how special your position is – you are able to zoom in on the oddities of a culture, a society, with the perspective of an outsider. You are accumulating experiences and insights that you share with very few people and that fewer would even know you've had. So don't forget to zoom out and look at the bigger picture. Place that pin on the map of the world and appreciate that with all difficulties incurred with living in a foreign country, your pin is one of its kind.

WHAT THE EXPERT SAYS

Married Plus Four, a Trail Between Four Countries

by LEIGH MATTHEWS

"Roots and wings" is the standout byline in Avivit's story about the Iranian Kurdish Jewish woman from Israel who marries the purebred Brit and together, in the hurricane of a globally mobile life, they give birth to, and raise, four children. Ambiguous as 'roots and wings' seems, the tolerance of ambiguity and flexibility required to be so is a hallmark of expat life; how else does one find place when out of place and how else does one tether intercultural spouses together or nurture children across cultures? Amongst so many others, several themes stand out from Avivit's story: culture shock, mothering kids without a village, the expat mother's two choice dilemma, the travails of the 'trailing' or 'accompanying spouse' and the journey of TCKs or Third Culture Kids.

Hopping from London, to Belgium, to Israel, to Paris, then London: highly mobile expats perceive these moves as opportunities for renewal, but there is no escape from the inevitable culture shock and labour of learning the lay of the land in each destination.

All expats ought to familiarise themselves with the four stages of culture shock outlined by anthropologist Kalervo Oberg. Phase one, the *Honeymoon Period*, the period of joy we signed up for, slips from bliss into the uncertainty and doubt, annoyance, and the loneliness and alienation of *Culture Shock*. In this Crisis Phase it is essential to seek out support, in addition to practising Mindful Self-compassion. A capacity to sit with discomfort and foster a resilient focus on how "this too shall pass" is required. The third phase is an upswing to *Adjustment* - familiarity with the locality, customs, the language and, a not entirely disillusioned outlook on the host culture. Stage four, *Mastery*, entails a navigation of a 'third space', a hybrid of *this* culture and *that* culture, a creation of one's own cultural milieu, and acceptance of difference without judgment. There is a peaceful co-existence of whatever works for you amongst all other possibilities without the need to damn any cultural nuance as right or wrong, good or bad.

The highly mobile family are a different creature altogether, on an expert level of resilience. As Avivit writes: the first year is for mapping the basics – schools, supermarkets, healthcare providers, services; the second year opens up space for friendships and, just as the third year promises a sort of settling, there is movement again. Linguistic ability, curiosity and openness, tolerance for uncertainty and ambiguity, patience and respect, a healthy ego, and a keen sense of humuor – these are the qualities required to adjust. No pressure! These *'cultural competencies'* that Schneider and Barsoux (2003) identified will also constitute the character of the TCK, both as a natural consequence of their diverse lived experience across cultural environments, and insofar as these qualities are cultivated by parents.

Avivit's children are not only TCKs, the children of

high mobility parents, they are also kids from bi/multi-cultural/multi-ethnic parents AND kids with mixed-racial heritage. Diversity of foods, languages, communities, landscapes and cultures is par for the course for TCKs. As Avivit writes of one of her four children: *"...everything we managed to pack into her eight years of life as part of an expat family – moving to four countries, speaking three languages, switching in and out of six houses and still not having a place to call home – had not caused confusion or muddled her identity. She sounded like a young citizen of the world, with a family travelling alongside her."*

Preparation of children for moves, whether in high or low mobility contexts, requires conscious connection with activities, family rituals, routines or things that provide predictability in the midst of transition. Embracing transitions, cultivating curiosity and a growth mindset, playing to enable kids to process their world; these are essential to help the TCK thrive. Family, community and place are "anchors and mirrors". They give children the *roots* to ground them but also reflect to children a sense of who they are despite the upheavals of a *winged life*. Families allow children to feel they matter, hold space and give permission for a child to feel and cultivate autonomy by offering choices.

With high mobility come endless goodbyes, seasoning the rich lived experiences of TCKs and their expat parents with grief and, especially for the TCKs, and the accompanying spouse, questions of belonging. Expat spouses are often required to make a choice: career and childcare for the children or choose to be the family anchor? Deborah chose her career and found ways to make this work as an enriching factor for her children;

Avivit chose to anchor and take whatever work options were available in the numerous locations she found herself living in. This is the life of the expat – impossible two-choice dilemmas in which there will always be a trade-off, a sacrifice of this or that. Then there is that other aspect of expat life, the sustaining part, that is a *this* AND *that* scenario: roots AND wings. Or, another way of thinking: expat families are like trees, with branches reaching out for new experiences yet with moveable roots, a sense of belonging nourished by each other.

"A tree has roots in the soil yet reaches to the sky. It tells us that in order to aspire we need to be grounded and that no matter how high we go it is from our roots that we draw sustenance."
Wangari Maathai

Useful resources

expatkidsclub.com/blog

expatparentingabroad.com

messageparis.org

bctbelgium.org

CHAPTER
FOUR

Bremain in Spain: a Brexit Legacy

SUE WILSON MBE
VALENCIA (SPAIN)

Sue Wilson, 67
At home, Alcossebre, Valencia

Photo by Loredana Boros

Originally from Oxford, Sue Wilson lived in London and Cambridge, working in sales, management and training. She moved to Spain in 2007 and worked as an English language teacher. Sue became Chair of Bremain in Spain – a group campaigning against Brexit – shortly after the 2016 referendum. As a pro-EU activist, she has been involved in many rallies and events and has worked closely with politicians and campaigners in Westminster and Brussels. Sue was lead plaintiff in the 'Wilson versus The Prime Minister' (Theresa May) legal challenge, over the validity of the Brexit referendum. Sue lives in the Valencian Community with her husband and four cats, and although officially retired, campaigns full-time for the protection of British citizens' rights across Spain and the EU. Sue was awarded an MBE in the 2021 Queen's Birthday Honours List for services to British Nationals in Spain and the European Union.

Bremain in Spain: a Brexit Legacy

I first visited Spain when I was 18. It was my first ever vacation without my parents and it was love at first sight. My reasons for falling for Spain then were very different from those I have now, but are probably typical of your average teenager. The weather and beaches were glorious, the drinks were enormous (and cheap) and the entertainment lasted all night.

Years later, after meeting my husband Steve, we became regular visitors to Spain, on both city breaks and coastal trips. Gradually the dream of a Spanish retirement started to take root.

After years of working long hours in demanding careers – me in Sales Management and Training, and Steve in IT – we started to consider buying a second home, to get our feet on the Spanish property ladder. In 2005, in our fifties, we began our search online, visiting different parts of the country virtually – some parts we knew and many we didn't.

With a plan to visit Spain several times a year, and in all seasons, we began narrowing our search area. We decided that the north would be too cold for us in winter, the south too hot in summer, so we planned an exploratory visit halfway down the east coast, to an area we knew nothing about – the Valencian Community. We spent two weeks in Alcossebre, with a view to travelling 100 kilometres north and south of our base, in order to find the perfect spot. It wasn't long before we realised that we were already there.

After viewing various properties, we soon realised we couldn't afford anything we liked without downsizing in the UK. We put down a deposit on an off-plan townhouse that was no more than an architect's drawing and a hole in the ground. By the time it was built two years later, we'd thrown our holiday-home plans out of the window and decided to move permanently to Spain instead. Why wait for retirement? Why not just take the plunge? It was the best decision we ever made.

When we arrived in Spain, Steve and I were determined to integrate into Spanish society. We avoided the hangouts of the British, intent not to live the stereotypical media version of 'expat' life. We were/are British of course, but being European, and adjusting to our new Spanish life was important to us both. Of course, everyone called us the 'new English neighbours' – a mistake my Scottish husband was quick to correct. Although we initially lived on a complex, we had few neighbours in the beginning. Most were Spanish second-homers, so were only around at weekends or for holidays. Many of the houses on the complex weren't even sold yet, so out of 80 homes, only six were occupied all year round.

For the first year I felt very lonely. I missed my family and close friends of course, but also I missed having a busy working day interacting with others. The only people we came into contact with initially were the estate and management agents and shop assistants. The lack of Spanish language skills didn't help us to settle either.

As we moved to Spain with few possessions and no furniture, the first few months were taken up with shopping. We had moved into a completely empty house, naively expecting it would have the basics. Little did we know we'd arrive to find no electricity or water connected and no light fittings – not even light bulbs. The first few weeks were little more than camping under a roof. It was a full six months before we had completely furnished the house and could live beyond just two rooms.

Despite having moved house numerous times, and to different cities, during our marriage, moving to another country was a much bigger upheaval. We had lots of visitors that first year, and I kept myself busy getting to know the lay of the land and working on my Spanish language skills. Gradually, we built up a network of friends and acquaintances and started to find our feet.

After a few scheduled months off, we both worked part-time for our old employers in the UK. I later found work in Spain as an English language teacher, before we both retired. I say I'm retired, but since the Brexit referendum in June 2016, I have never worked so hard, or such long hours, in my entire career.

Before that fateful day, when the referendum turned my world upside down, I had never been very interested in current affairs, and most definitely not in politics. I used to complain that Steve was always watching the news – partly because it bored me, but also because I didn't understand it or care to do so. When friends talked politics, I never engaged – I lacked the confidence to comment, or never felt I knew enough to offer an opinion.

That all started to change as the day of the Brexit referendum loomed closer. I started to worry that the UK was about to make a terrible decision and vote to shoot itself in the foot. I had no real idea what leaving the EU might mean for us Brits living in Europe, or the UK, but it could hardly be good!

Against my better judgement, I stayed up all night to watch the results come in, hoping to be proved wrong, only to be proved right. I broke down in tears at 6am when the result was confirmed, feeling totally overwhelmed by events, and in shock. It felt like a nightmare come to life, and I just wanted to wake up and find it had all been a bad dream.

For the next three weeks, I felt a range of emotions usually associated with grief. I have never been a person to get angry or lose my self-control. Before the referendum, I could have counted the times I had ever lost my temper in single figures. In one fell swoop, Brexit had changed all that – it had turned me into someone I didn't recognise. It was a rollercoaster of fear, anger, depression, shock, disbelief and sadness. And swearing, a lot of swearing! I would fly off the handle at nothing, then burst into tears for no apparent reason. I didn't stop crying for three whole weeks, regardless of where I was or who I was with. I must have received some very strange looks in the local supermarket! Even now, I can't fully explain why it affected me so deeply, or still does.

The only thing that brought any relief in the early days was talking to close friends that were feeling exactly the same. No explanations were necessary – every emotion, every day, was a shared experience. Nothing else seemed to matter – Brexit was our sole topic of conversation.

On day 22, the first day without tears, I woke up determined to act. I joined the anti-Brexit campaign group Bremain in Spain. I needed to get involved and take personal action. I don't know where that drive came from, but I began devouring the news. I became very active online, engaging with like-minded people and benefitting from their support. It was enormously comforting to realise that the feelings I was struggling to deal with were shared by others. The group's members would talk openly about their feelings of helplessness and shock, but also would offer words of comfort to others in the same boat.

It was a combination of therapy and the comfort in knowing that I was doing something, not just wallowing in despair. Within three months, I was invited to take over as Chair of Bremain, and I have dedicated my life to it ever since. It's an obsession. I'm not sure my sanity would have survived intact without it. I had found a new family.

The fact that Bremain was a 'Remainers' only forum encouraged our members to open up. In other forums where 'Remainers' and 'Leavers' were mixed together, conversations often turned to arguments and at times, the level of vitriol could be toxic. Little effort was made, in those early days, to understand the opposing point of view, but especially when Brexit was being venerated by Brits who live beside us. The oft-repeated 'fact' that nothing was going to change for those of us living in Spain, is as ridiculous now as it was then.

One of the most difficult aspects to deal with was how Brexit was causing rifts between friends, and worse still, between families. We began to look on those we thought we knew, that had voted for Brexit, in a completely different light. How could they have been taken in? How could they betray us? Many looked for someone to blame. That blame was often misdirected at those that had been lied to, rather than those that had lied to them. Sadly, many of those rifts between friends and families have never healed, even after all this time. Some never will.

There are so many downsides to Brexit, but on a personal level, there have been some positives too. The people I have met have certainly been the highlight. As Bremain became more established, it's been my privilege to work with some of the kindest, most dedicated and caring people I have ever known. The Bremain council, and many of our volunteers, have become close friends, most especially my second in command, John. Despite the relatively short length of time we've known each other, the intense shared experience, fighting for what we believe in, has created lifelong bonds of friendship with many kindred spirits. Pro-EU campaigning has brought me into contact with some amazing people from all walks of life, many of whom I would never have met under any other circumstances.

Since the 2016 referendum I have closely followed events in Westminster and Brussels, and built a network of contacts – both politicians and activists. Visiting the European Parliament was always an amazing experience – a whole village of Europeans, speaking in several different languages but all working together for the common good. Westminster was always interesting too, but it definitely lacked the European vibe.

My first experience of meeting politicians, in January 2017, was when I was offered the opportunity to present to MP Hilary Benn's 'Exiting the EU Select Committee' in the Houses of Parliament. I presented evidence regarding healthcare for British citizens living in the EU, and I have never been so nervous in my entire life! So nervous, in fact, that I had to put my glass of water down as my hand was shaking so much I thought I would spill it –

thankfully, that wasn't obvious on the video recording. The opportunity enabled me to meet citizens' rights campaigners from the Netherlands, France, Germany and Italy.

When the first anti-Brexit march and rally was planned in London, there was no question in my mind – of course I was going, and with many members of the Bremain family. I was delighted to be asked to make a speech, although I had no experience of public speaking on that scale. As a manager, I had regularly spoken to groups of 10-30 people, but delivering a speech to 120,000 people was a whole different ball game. Nerve-wracking yes, but the crowd was so receptive – I was, after all, preaching to the converted – and I got a real buzz from it. According to Steve, hand me a microphone now, and you'll get crushed in the stampede to the stage!

My Brexit journey has changed me in ways I could never have imagined. Apart from discovering a temper I never knew existed, I'm also a lot more confident. I have always been an extrovert, and it's not that I lacked confidence before, but learning new skills has certainly broadened my horizons. I guess you can teach an old dog new tricks after all. Apart from the public speaking, I've got better at dealing with confrontation and I've become a writer of sorts. I now write a weekly article for an English language newspaper in Spain and have occasionally written for UK publications, or provided quotes to journalists. Considering my previous nervousness about voicing any political opinions, it still tickles me when journalists seek out my comment on current affairs.

The emotional rollercoaster has been with me throughout the Brexit experience, although my average day of campaigning is a calmer affair now. The highs and lows have come largely when there have been major developments. The highs have included: seeing former UK PM Theresa May lose her majority; coming very close to securing a second referendum; postponing Brexit day; and especially the rallies and marches. The lows have included the 2019 general election, the Brexit divorce agreement finally being voted through parliament, and of course, Brexit day on 31st January 2020.

It is difficult to remember how European I felt before Brexit – I took being European for granted. Despite having taken advantage of the benefits that EU membership offered, I am not sure that I was fully aware that I had the EU to thank for those benefits. Being European just came naturally. The thought of losing that EU citizenship is heart-breaking. The thought of being British, and being associated with what Britain is becoming, just fills me with shame. In my first speech in London, I said I hoped that one day I'd be proud to be British again. I'm still waiting, and the prospect seems more remote than ever.

I don't think we fully appreciated what Spanish life for us would be like when we originally made our plans to emigrate. After years of Spanish holidays, part of you imagines that living in Spain will be like an extended vacation. At times, it feels that way – the climate allows us to live differently, spending much more time outdoors. But normal life in Spain is just that – normal. It involves going to work, grocery shopping, doing laundry, car maintenance, housework and all those other everyday activities that you leave behind when you go on holiday.

Even during that first year of adjustment, we never

regretted our decision to make Spain our home. In fact, if we have any regrets, it's that we didn't see the light sooner. At least our delay meant we both worked in the UK long enough to qualify for a full UK pension, so now we are both retired and mortgage free, and completely secure.

When we dreamed of our retirement in Spain, we never imagined that I would be doing voluntary work seven days a week. I am often asked how much longer I intend to continue campaigning, or what I will do when Brexit is finally all over. It's a difficult question to answer, and it changes depending on circumstances.

On the one hand, and despite all the pain, disappointment and effort, I am doing something that I care about deeply, and which, despite everything, I enjoy. I have a supportive husband who gets pleasure from seeing me so motivated and engaged, and he's proud of what I have achieved. That means so much to me. On the other hand, I'm now in my late 60s, full-time campaigning is exhausting, and Steve and I deserve that retirement we dreamed of.

There have been many times I've looked ahead and given myself a deadline. I'll give up Bremain when Brexit is 'done'. I'll give up Bremain when the transition period comes to an end. Then something will happen in Westminster or Brussels, and the adrenalin will kick in again, and any thoughts of quitting go out of the window. Not to mention the fact that Brexit likely won't be fully over for a decade. The negotiations are likely to be going on for many years, and at some point there'll be a major campaign for the UK to re-join the EU. Can I bear not to be involved in that? Maybe I should let fate decide and give up Bremain when a Brexiter finally gives me one real benefit of Brexit. I might have a very long wait!

How do you give up an obsession? Find another to replace it? With these new campaigning skills I've acquired, it seems a shame not to put them to good use. Yet, despite my caring about things like animal welfare, or the environment, will they ever spark the passion in me that Brexit has? Ask me again tomorrow. Or the next day. I can't guarantee you'll get the same answer twice.

REFLECTIONS

Bremain in Spain: a Brexit Legacy

by SUE WILSON MBE

Moving house can be a traumatic experience, moving country even more so. But it can also be an opportunity to reinvent yourself, to broaden your horizons and to live a new and exciting life. In order to make the best of it, here are my recommendations.

Put yourself out there. Moving to another town where you don't know anyone can be daunting. Moving to a country where English is not the first language can increase one's sense of isolation and loneliness. Keeping in regular contact with friends and family you have left behind will help. However, it is important to make new friends and acquaintances, but cautiously. If you are feeling particularly lonely, there's a temptation to rush into new relationships that may be short-lived. Far better to find things to do that you enjoy – walking, going to the gym, dance classes, reading, playing golf etc – and join local groups that share your interests.

New life, new you. Creating a new home in a new country is an opportunity to create a new you. If, like me, you move somewhere with a significantly different climate, the weather alone will change your daily habits.

Embrace the changes and explore how they can improve your lifestyle and behaviour. Whether it is a walk along the beach, a few hours gardening, or just reading on the balcony, a better climate will encourage you to spend more time outdoors. Don't be afraid to try healthy new habits or give up old bad ones. I gave up smoking when I moved to Spain, and 14 years later, I'm still free of the tobacco habit. I also took up campaigning, having discovered a passion for politics that I would never have imagined possible. It's never too late – or too early – to reinvent yourself, and the journey can be quite exhilarating.

Never underestimate yourself. As you come to grips with a new life, new home, new job, new friends, you might initially feel a little overwhelmed. No doubt there will be days when you miss those you left behind or miss elements of your old life that didn't travel. You might miss a favourite food, favourite restaurant or favourite shop. You might even wonder whether you have made a big mistake in upping sticks and moving abroad in the first place. No matter the cause of any unsettled feelings, remember, they are not because you lack the skill or the will to make your new life work. You may not feel particularly brave, but don't underestimate the scale of the task that you have just undertaken, or the level of optimism and bravery that was required to do what you have done. Be proud of the courage you have shown and know that you have it in you to make a better, healthier, and likely a longer life, because of it.

Travel light. In an effort to make yourself feel at home in a new environment, there will be a strong temptation to take as much of your old lives with you as possible. Don't. Take things of sentimental value but leave the furniture and the baggage behind. It's just stuff, and it likely won't fit in your new home or your new life. Leaving so much behind can be immensely liberating and allows you to start a new life with a clean slate. It also allows you to build a new home to fit that new, and different, life. Take your time to fill your new home, as you take time to fill your new life. The shape of the future is yours to decide and there's no need to rush, as long as you have a bed to sleep in.

Be open to new opportunities. My new-found interest in politics, and fighting for the protection of our rights, was not a road I had ever expected to travel. Not only did I lack the interest in current affairs, but I lacked the confidence to discuss them. If my Brexit journey has taught me anything, it's that we never truly know what we are capable of until we put ourselves outside our comfort zone. I had thought that moving to Spain might be the most adventurous thing I would do in my lifetime. In fact, it was merely the beginning of a challenging and exciting journey, picking up new skills along the way.

Despite a few teething problems and personal adjustments, I have never regretted my move to Spain. I am so glad that I decided not to wait until retirement to make it happen, and now I am retired, I am more settled, more at home, and happier than I have ever been. In part, that is due to this wonderful country, its friendly and welcoming people and a climate that takes me out of my home and out of myself. But it is also due to changes to my skillset, my confidence levels and my newly discovered passion. No matter what age you are when you take that step, make it count. You will never have a better opportunity to transform your life, and yourself. Grasp it with both hands!

WHAT THE EXPERT SAYS

Bremain in Spain: a Brexit Legacy

by LEIGH MATTHEWS

Retirement was the primary motivation for moving abroad for 4% of expat respondents in the Internations Expat Insider 2020 Survey. Some expats fall in love with a place and harbour their dream of moving abroad throughout their life, some expats look to moving abroad to support a better quality of life fuelled by a lower cost of living. Whatever the reason, and at whatever time in our life, the transition abroad will always present a variety of unique challenges.

Planning is essential to aid the leap that is moving to another country as Sue and Steve did – narrowing the search area, visiting the country beforehand, checking out real estate, searching online and even visiting parts of the country virtually. A resource to kick off your research around which country you'd like to retire to is *Expat Exchange*, with stories of retirees living in various parts of the world and a cost of living calculator. Check out *Retirement Reimagined* for a step-by-step support through the process. *International Living* is another resource for exploring the possibility of retirement abroad.

Once you have everything mapped out, you're good to go. Or, are you? Sue reflects on the surprising impact: *"Despite having moved house numerous times, and to different cities... moving to another country was a much bigger upheaval."* A startlingly high proportion of expats fail to prepare for the psychological impact of the disruption of expatriation. Loneliness, loss of support networks and activities, erasure of the safety of the familiar, and the stressors of establishing a life abroad can be major burdens to bear. Culture shock can feel much like depression and anxiety. Language barriers can feel like a cage of isolation. Identity comes into question: Who am I? Where is home? Do I want to fit in and how can I do that without losing my culture and identity? The abrasion of your host country's cultural nuances and differences can leave you feeling frustrated and regretful. Preparing for the inevitable roller coaster ride of shocks by speaking with an expat therapist or coach is highly recommended. An expat therapist can help you understand what to expect on your expat journey and what strategies and tools can help to mitigate the pain and prevent you from internalising the issues or turning to alcohol as a coping strategy, creating further suffering for yourself.

Though expat life comes with numerous emotional and logistical challenges, it will also likely take you in enriching directions you could never have imagined. This is the story of Sue, who has unexpectedly become a bastion of the Bremain movement in Spain. *"It was with a combination of therapy and the comfort of knowing I was doing something, not just wallowing in despair"*, she writes. While she enjoys her life as an expat, she finds meaning in her fight for her right to be a citizen of the EU, rather than being limited to Britain. In a recent United Nations report, it was estimated that the EU held 1.2 million Brexpats – British citizens resident in other European Union countries. Brexit has been an unexpected and shocking blow to British citizens who are EU expats and retirees. Britain has rejected its citizens' right to freedom of movement in the EU concomitant with its rejection of immigration into its own country. There are a plethora of issues surrounding UK pensions, driving licences, registration as permanent residents, access to healthcare, being limited to 90 days in second residences – many lament they no longer have the best of both worlds as a Brexpat in the EU.

Useful resources

Brexit: What the hell happens next? by Ian Dunt

How to stop Brexit (& make Britain great again) by Nick Clegg

The Brexshit Book: A Remainer's Self-help Guide to Leaving the EU by Steven Stevens

Retirement Reimagined: From Ordinary to Extraordinary by Dr Terry NyHuis

bremaininspain.com (Bremain in Spain)

ecreu.com (Expat Citizens Right in EU)

brexpatshov.com (Brexpats)

expatexchange.com

internationalliving.com

CHAPTER
FIVE

Poms in Thongs:
an Aussie Culture Shock

ANNABEL COTTON
SYDNEY (AUSTRALIA)

Annabel Cotton, 51
Fairlight Foreshore, Sydney

Photo by Josh Cotton

Annabel Cotton is a former teacher and radio journalist from the UK now based in Australia. She moved to Sydney in 1998, where she continued her career working at the national broadcasters ABC and SBS. She and her British husband settled on Sydney's Northern Beaches and went on to have three children: Josh, Jamie and Ella. After some time at home, she returned to the workforce as a history guide at the site of Australia's first Quarantine Station before changing direction to work in the library service. She now lives in the seaside suburb of Manly with her husband Dan, their three children, dog Luna and cat, Fats.

Poms in Thongs:
an Aussie Culture Shock

"The Aussie customs officer asked me if I had a criminal record, I said I didn't think you needed one these days!" My Dad relished delivering this hackneyed line the first time he flew into Sydney.

The old convict gags and culture jokes probably would have made me laugh back in the day. But 22 years on, they make me cringe; while I'm still a Brit, I also count myself an Australian. (And incidentally we have more than 50,000 years of incredible culture in this country: Aboriginal art predates Turner by 50 millennia).

Assimilation, however, didn't come as easily as I anticipated. Moving here in 1998, I expected Australia to be a home away from home; only with much better weather and great beaches. I mean, we shared the same language, similar values, customs and the same Queen, how different could it be for goodness sake?!

My curiosity about Australia was initially piqued by watching the film 'Walkabout' as a teenager. It centres on a schoolgirl lost in the Australian outback who is befriended and guided by a young Aboriginal boy. I couldn't fathom a country with endless skies and landscapes so vast that there were still areas on which not a soul had set foot. I still marvel at this 'wide brown land', so enormous that it straddles three different time zones.

12 years later I found myself on honeymoon here; a secret recce to see if I liked Sydney enough to emigrate. 10 days in tropical Far North Queensland and a week in Sydney in the Aussie mid-winter, was enough to sell it to me. We applied on the points system for permanent residency via a migration consultant. My husband Dan is in finance and at the time I was a radio journalist. It was a very binary process in the late 1990s; you were more likely to score points for a vocational qualification that related to your profession. So, hilariously to me, as a poorly paid radio journalist, I scored more points than Dan who earned considerably more. He was a Cambridge graduate but had no vocational qualification linked to his job. I had a degree in English but then completed a postgraduate diploma in radio journalism, which did correlate with my job. As the laconic Aussie migration consultant explained; a stripper with a dance diploma was technically more likely to be offered residency than Bill Gates, who has no formal IT qualification.

It was a wrench to leave the UK, but we decided it would probably only be for a couple of years. We had a very comfortable life; great family, friends, a small house outside London and good jobs. It was the era of Cool Britannia, Britpop and a sense of optimism with the newly anointed PM Tony Blair. There was no real motivation to leave other than itchy feet, the weather (of course), and an urge to experience something different. A travel TV ad at the time featured a couple at the kitchen table. One said to the other "I wish we had gone to Australia 20 years ago".

Finally, after some 10 months, we received news of our visa application. It was like opening exam results. The letter, containing the Australian government logo of a coat of arms held up by a kangaroo and emu, stated quite simply that pending reference checks our application had been successful.

While we were excited, it was a huge, scary wake-up call. We took a deep breath and weighed up the pros and cons of uprooting our lives from a familiar city to a completely alien one at the other end of world; with no jobs, no family and no friends. We agreed we didn't want regrets and 'what ifs' peppering our conversation in later life. We decided we had to at least give it a go.

After an exhausting round of goodbye gatherings, we finally packed up, rented out the house and headed for Sydney. We arrived in Sydney late February to a shiny, palm tree fringed city with its impossibly blue harbour; the air heavy with heat, humidity and the heady fragrance of frangipani. Initial exhilaration and euphoria soon gave way to reality. Dan had come down with the flu, it was 36 degrees and we were pounding the pavements looking for a flat while living out of a suitcase in a cheap downtown hotel. Fortunately at the time, Sydney was affordable – rents were relatively cheap compared to London (now it's one of the world's most expensive cities). We started off in the pricey suburb of Darling Point; the flat was basic, frequented by cockroaches, but had mesmerising views of the harbour and was a 10-minute ferry ride into the Central Business District.

After the initial excitement of getting to know the city, I fell into a down patch. While Dan had managed to tee up a job within 10 days of our arrival, I was struggling to find work. It seemed my experience working for radio stations in the UK did not open the doors I expected. It took some three months before I managed to get shifts as a casual journalist at ABC radio, the national broadcaster.

Up to that point, I struggled to fill my days. While Dan interacted with colleagues at work, I stayed home in a sparsely furnished, stinking hot flat for ten hours waiting for a phone to be connected or furniture to be delivered. I was really beginning to feel the distance. The internet was in its infancy, so apart from the odd email, it took a weekly expensive phone call, fitted around an 11 hour time difference, to keep in touch. Despite no language barrier, life felt very lonely in those early months. It wasn't a loneliness associated with physical solitude, but more one from lacking genuine human connections of any depth. I had left behind not only family, but treasured friendships going back decades. There's an ease to these female kinships, a comfort in knowing one another's 'baggage'. Now I felt really exposed; feeling an urgency to impress and sell myself to try and forge new relationships.

Desperate times called for desperate measures. We had been given a few phone numbers of Aussie-based friends of friends back home. I took a deep breath and brightly made phone calls to complete strangers asking them out for drinks. Fortunately one of my closest friends was snared this way. Despite a busy job in banking, she would call me regularly to see if I could 'fit in' a lunch, knowing full well how empty my schedule was. She had no idea how much I would look forward to these catch-ups.

The loneliness bubble had burst. We began to have a broader social circle and a busy calendar going to barbeques, bars and eating out.

The food and coffee in Sydney were an absolute revelation. Jamie Oliver was only just taking off in the

UK and jacket potatoes with beans/chilli/cheese was still the staple of most lunch menus there. Here a whole new world of Asian and fusion cuisine opened up to us. I tried my first sushi, mistaking the wasabi for avocado and nearly self-combusting. Coffee here was like a religion – and we remain dedicated followers.

In the early days there was a lot to understand. Australia is renowned for its 'critters'; from the venomous Sydney funnel web spider to the beautiful but deadly blue-ringed octopus. Add to that multiple breeds of shark, 170 different types of snake along with lethal jellyfish and no wonder international visitors set foot with some trepidation on Aussie soil. But 'the critters' get a bad press. Really. Injuries and deaths from these creatures are often sensationalised.

That said, they are around. A friend of mine had a frighteningly close encounter with a snake after one slid into the passenger side of her car while she was emptying groceries in her suburban driveway. Horrified, she opened all the doors and left the car for a couple of days, hoping the snake would make an exit. A few days later, after thorough inspection, she decided it must have slithered away. It was as she was driving along a busy dual carriageway that the skinny serpent popped its head out of the air conditioning vent. Barely pausing to think, she pulled over, grabbed a stick from the side of the road, allowed the snake to curl itself around it, and then flicked it out of the window.

We have other less menacing visitors to our garden; the ubiquitous possum, which sounds like a small infantry division marching across our roof; the long-nosed bandicoot, a small nocturnal marsupial; and an array of colourful, screeching birds which display all the contrasts of the place, flashing crimson beauty with a noise that would make milk turn sour.

The drama of the weather was something else... the heat... ah the heat. I had never experienced sun like it; I had basted myself on European beaches for years, often getting minor sunburn in the process. But the Australian sun is unforgiving; I soon learned why you **always** 'slip on a shirt, slop on sunscreen and slap on a hat', a line from a Cancer Council campaign which has been drummed into the Aussie psyche. Schoolchildren are subject to the blanket rule of 'no hat no play'. One year, this rule was not observed at the 'book parade' at my son's school. It was always held outside in the winter as the weather is generally mild. The children all dress as their favourite characters; Josh decided to be the lion from 'The Lion, the Witch and the Wardrobe', so was fully kitted out as a furry big cat. The day was unseasonably hot and hit 30 degrees. He got heatstroke. (My bad.)

We have woken up to blood-red skies, choking smoke and black embers raining down on the beaches from bushfires, leaving a black band three metres wide at low tide. We have watched in awe as rain, the like of which I have never seen, has fallen in great cascades and have had our car almost written off by hailstones the size of cricket balls.

But the biggest danger here is the surf. The reality is that a fatal shark attack is a far 'sexier' story than a death by drowning. The beaches are magnificent but present very dangerous conditions for those not accustomed to strong rips (currents). Tourists often panic and try to swim against the rip, which ultimately exhausts you and leaves you no closer to shore. Strangely, what you should do is swim **with** the current. When its power diminishes, swim across and out, **then** back into shore. Very Australian – take the contrary view, go with the flow and you'll succeed.

One of the appealing aspects of settling here was the more relaxed approach to life. While the casual 'no worries' attitude is a cliché, frankly it can be seen as a national characteristic. This informality feeds into the vernacular too – if an Aussie can shorten a word or a name, they will. Sometimes even abbreviations are abbreviated – the MCG (Melbourne Cricket Ground) is known simply as 'the G'. Garbage men are garbos, politicans are pollies, paramedics are ambos, tradesmen are tradies. "Mate, I'll be devo if we can't get some tinnies and maccas at the footy this arvo, maybe just grab a sanga from the servo?" Translation: "Friend, I'll be sorely disappointed if we can't have a beer and some McDonald's at the rugby this afternoon, maybe we'll just grab a sandwich from the petrol station?"

This informal nature is further reflected in the casual attitude to dress. I have been fighting a losing battle for years to try and get my sons to put on a collared shirt when we eat out. It took some time to adjust to the relaxed national dress code and the fact that you can wear boardies (boardshorts) and thongs (flip flops) to the Opera House if you so choose. Frankly, in the summer I'm surprised to see my kids wearing any footwear, even when going to the shops.

When I first moved to Australia, I spent a lot of energy trying to stay connected with the political and cultural landscape back in the UK; the Australian system and characters were so unfamiliar. Australians do have a bit of a chip on their shoulders about the yoke of their British colonial past. While there is a Republican movement, there's also widespread apathy and disagreement about what model a Head of State should take. I used to slavishly follow the news in the UK and didn't make the effort to connect with what was happening in Australia: with three tiers of politics; federal, state and local it was a lot to wrap my head around. It's not even that the news reporting is parochial; Australians are big travellers and are engaged with the world. But when we first came here, there was still a sense of 'cultural cringe'; Australians seemed to do a lot of navel-gazing; reflecting on what it meant to be Australian, obsessively wanting to know how others perceive their country.

The year after we arrived 25% of Queenslanders voted for the staunchly anti-immigration Pauline Hanson, who is still a Senator. But many of Australia's success stories are third generation Jewish refugees or second generation Vietnamese. There's huge controversy about how refugees are treated – with polarised views from compassionate to obdurate. Aboriginal people have a shorter life expectancy, higher rates of infant mortality and lower levels of education and employment than non-indigenous Australians.

The economy has been propped up by coal and iron ore for a century. This ensured no recession since the 1930s – until Covid-19 hit. The obsession with sport sees the arts grossly under-funded, meanwhile (some) cricketers cheat and rugby league players are lauded, while their sporting bodies overlook domestic violence, drug use and alcoholism. But on the other hand, Australian women's sport is exemplary in its successes.

So it is a place of infuriating and fascinating polarity, and strange happenings.

It was falling pregnant here that really helped me put down roots. After three years we had our first child in an excellent public hospital. Of course, as any parent will tell you, that was the easy bit. Not having any family to navigate motherhood was hard. My lifeline came in the form of a group of women I connected with who had babies a similar age. We became a tight-knit circle of friends, some of whom are among my closest to this day. The unifying factor was that we all had family overseas or interstate, at least a plane ride away. We baby-sat for each other, had cooking rosters when siblings were born and partied hard on rare nights away from the kids.

I'm aware of the pain I caused my mother by choosing to have a family so far away. While she never openly criticised our decision to emigrate, I know that she laboured under a quiet grief about it. If I'm honest, it fundamentally changed our relationship; my mother never expressed it, but I know that she was hurt at my decision. It took nearly three years and the birth of her first grandson to get her to visit. Meanwhile, I harboured a deep-seated guilt but also a resentment that she wouldn't endorse our move. This gnawed away at me; eventually it took attending a self-help style programme to have an epiphany of sorts and come to a level of acceptance about my life choices.

This was especially hard when it became clear that my mother was beginning a slow descent into dementia. My father remained resolutely in denial about it for a number of years; always trying to cover up her memory failings. Their trips out here became less frequent. On one visit she wandered off from us in my local town centre and was found slumped in full sun on a hot metal bench. When she came around she thought she was on holiday in France. Most upsetting was one trip back to the UK when Mum was at the height of her confusion. I was sat next to her at a family dinner when she asked me where I lived. "Australia!" she exclaimed, "Oh I have a daughter who lives there". I made my excuses, went to the bathroom and quietly wept; I was already grieving my mother's loss before she had gone. Before she died in 2016, I had flown back four times in just over a year as her condition worsened.

Moving here brought me closer to my father, however, who fully supported our move to Sydney and loved the outdoor lifestyle we had adopted. After caring for my mother for years, Dad seemed to find a new lease of life after she passed away; flying to Australia on his own in consecutive years at the age of 85 and 86. He loved the breakfast cultural mismatch 'combo' of Turkish bread, vegemite and a flat white. And he adored sitting outside in the sunshine, decimating our small stock of full-blooded Aussie Shiraz.

Despite the distance, we have made a big effort to stay connected with family. We have done that cursed flight many times, with crawling babies and rampaging toddlers; armed with fists full of lego and vials of Phenergan. I once did the journey alone with my two-year-old while five months pregnant. As we walked down the sky bridge to board the plane for 24 hours of misery, he excitedly enquired, "Are we at England now?" Changing explosive nappies at 30,000 feet in a toilet the size of a postage stamp, while being buffeted by turbulence, is an unforgettable experience. Travelling long haul with young children is right up there with childbirth on the pain scale. It reduced my usually mild-mannered husband to swearing at a Qantas hostess. She officiously reprimanded him for walking beyond the business class curtain momentarily, hours into pacing around the cabin with a distraught, overtired toddler. As for any sleep, forget it. Perhaps I should have knocked back the Phenergan bottle myself.

We took the opportunity to become citizens as soon as we could, a few years after arriving. I was taken aback at how emotional I found the experience. To my utter embarrassment I would later find myself regularly choking up at the national anthem at school assemblies. And yet both of us had found any flag-waving rendition of 'God Save the Queen' back in the UK acutely cringeworthy. Somehow the Australian national anthem tapped into an emotion; a pride that I had grown to love this country, with all its foibles, and was privileged to make it my home. It was an endorsement of the risk we had taken.

For more than two decades we have chosen to settle in the beachside suburb of Manly, a 20-minute ferry ride from the city. Dan was once late for work due to a whale migrating south holding up the boat. I left my career in radio journalism and stayed home while our three children were small. I returned to work at one of the oldest colonial sites in Sydney; a former Quarantine Station, where I took school groups around on history tours. It holds a mirror up to the Australian migration experience; from the earliest convict times in the early 1800s through to the post-war 'Populate or Perish' campaign attracting an influx of Europeans. On my most memorable day there, an Aboriginal smoking ceremony was being held on one end of the beach while an Islamic school at the other end performed their midday prayers. Standing on the stunning headland, I would often reflect on my own migration story and imagine those who had journeyed before me in much harsher circumstances.

Two decades after our arrival, the inexorable rise of technology has been a huge bonus for us to connect with the northern hemisphere. Until 2020, we always had the comfort of knowing we were only 24 hours away. Covid-19 dealt that a crushing blow. Australia closed its international borders in March of that year, implementing enforced quarantine in hotels for all international arrivals. This had the desired effect of keeping Covid-19 numbers relatively low, but has been a source of much anguish for people with families overseas. I consider myself very fortunate that my father passed away in January that year while I was still able to fly back for his funeral. Many others endured the wrench of losing a parent and not being able to leave the country.

When we lived in London we took its incredible history for granted, along with European holiday destinations on our doorstep. Now, it's the architecture of Europe that I miss most, along with late, light summer evenings (when it's warm), birdsong and pubs without the miserable Australian infection of the ubiquitous 'pokie' (slot) machine.

They say that emigration has four emotional stages to it: the honeymoon period, frustration, adjustment and adaptation. I am happily ensconced in stage four. For me, this country offers unparalleled and unique beauty, with Sydney providing an urban centre where nature and cosmopolitan city life happily collide. We live footsteps from stunning harbour beaches fringed by national park, with excellent restaurants and coffee shops close by. Further afield we have encountered the raw beauty of the red dirt of the Kimberley, incredible Aboriginal rock carvings in the Northern Territory and the magnificence of Queensland's Great Barrier Reef. But this is of course only barely scratching the surface of this vast continent.

I'm grateful we took up this challenge and that we are not living a life of regrets and 'what ifs'. Getting to this stage hasn't always been easy, but to be honest, if you ask me what I miss most about living in England (other than friends and family), I'd have to say... France.

REFLECTIONS

Poms in Thongs:
an Aussie Culture Shock

by ANNABEL COTTON

Moving abroad can be rewarding, liberating and terrifying all at once. I only began to really feel at home in Australia when I stopped counting the number of years and days I had been living here.

Do your homework. What are the visa requirements for your adopted country? Which areas will suit you best to live, in relation to where you are going to work? How does the healthcare/education/property/tax/political system work? What are the requirements for driving? The more you understand the fundamentals of your new home, the easier it will be to build your life there.

Have realistic expectations. If you think your time abroad will be one of 'living the dream', then dream on. People emigrate for a myriad of reasons: to take on new jobs, pursue new relationships or simply for new experiences. While your adopted country may be considered by many to be a glamorous holiday destination, the mundanity of the daily grind of chores and bureaucracy can be the same wherever you live. Don't underestimate the paperwork involved in setting yourself up. After the initial exhilaration and excitement of your big move, you will need to find strategies to manage the inevitable homesickness that follows. Much like grief, it comes at you in waves and just when you think you're over it, a sensory trigger like a smell or a particular song can bring on a visceral ache for 'home'. For me, hearing birdsong or church bells still takes me back to an English summer's morning or a French village square. Keep yourself busy and accept that this will happen, perhaps to a lesser degree the longer you live abroad, but possibly always. Wherever you choose to set up your new life, you're always going to have an accent, no matter how great your language or mimicry skills.

Don't get stuck in an expat social circle. There is an intangible bond between expats from the same country but don't let that become a crutch. It's great to connect with people who can help you navigate unfamiliar territory but find ways to meet local people: join a sport or social club, sign up to an evening class. I joined a local drama school after moving to Sydney and it was one of the best things I could have done. Have a baby! Not always practicable or realistic, but having children is one of the easiest ways to meet people and put down roots.

Immerse yourself. Embrace the rhythms of the country by really getting to know the bones of it. As an expat there is so much cultural history and baggage that we simply don't know. I moved to Australia before the digital age had kicked in so there were few online resources for expats. That landscape has changed hugely so use it. Devour as much material as you can that has a local focus: read newspapers and feature articles, read history and fiction, watch dramas, listen to the radio and go to the theatre. This is, of course, far less challenging in an English-speaking country like Australia, yet even here, there were references, idioms and abbreviations that left me completely flummoxed. Take on your new country's traditions, whether that be eating certain meals on particular days or observing a national day of remembrance. Where possible and practicable, become a citizen. To fully participate in Australian society, I felt the need to become a citizen and have the right to vote. This was an easy choice for me as I was able to keep my British passport and have dual nationality. I accept that this isn't possible for most expats.

Own your choices. You will inevitably miss out on some major life events: births, weddings and even funerals. This can leave you labouring under a weighty burden of guilt about the choices you've made. This may even be exacerbated by family members or friends, who have not made this path easy for you. You may not be able to change their attitudes, so change your own. Build a healthy relationship with your new country – stop bagging it out over what it lacks. Stop comparing; embrace the differences and look for the positives in your new home. Live in the moment; try not to constantly video-chat with friends and family. Accept that you may always feel a pull in both directions. For most people, leaving family and close friends is by far the most difficult feature of an expat life. This can be particularly hard and even traumatic during periods of ill health, grief or the early years of having children. You will inevitably feel a pull back 'home'. There will be deep connections and affection for both homelands; I firmly believe it is possible to have a fulfilled life, with a foot in each.

WHAT THE EXPERT SAYS

Poms in Thongs:
an Aussie Culture Shock

by LEIGH MATTHEWS

What is it like to get caught in a rip?

"Tourists often panic and try to swim against the rip, which ultimately exhausts you and leaves you no closer to shore. Strangely, what you should do is swim with the current. When its power diminishes, swim across and out, then back into shore. Very Australian – take the contrary view, go with the flow and you'll succeed."

Annabel's story is the story of expats who reach the mastery phase in their cultural adjustment, but not before dealing with the strong currents of culture shock: much like the currents or 'rips' on Australian beaches. Unlike tourists, expats stop swimming against the current, they adapt to the flow of their adopted culture. They don't necessarily lose what they bring with them, they integrate what works from both cultures.

Surviving a rip starts before you enter the water. Knowing how to swim, knowing what a rip looks like, knowing a calm surface can be deceptive, these are relevant skills for cultural adjustment too. Annabel's is a journey from Britain to Australia, from one English-speaking culture to another. Heading to a new locale with the expectation that the people will be the same, especially if the language is the same as your mother tongue, will leave you unprepared and disappointed. Settling into English-speaking countries as opposed to countries where citizens speak another language entirely, can be harder. The networks in place for expats may be fewer with the assumption that it will be easier for English-speaking immigrants to fit in. Managing expectations is important – expecting life to be mostly the same with minimal adjustment is a mistake. Annabel's story, although one of moving to an English-speaking country, also encompasses the hardships of the early emotional journey of any expat: distance, exhaustion, desperation, exposure, loneliness.

To leave everything and everyone familiar behind means to encounter an acute sense of vulnerability and isolation. This is the turmoil the expat gets caught in, much like the current or the 'rip' on the Aussie beach. In this season of expat life, the crisis phase, the culture shock, it can be tempting to swim against the current, to reject the host culture and values, to grip those of your passport culture, to create a hierarchy of culture and values: "mine is better than yours, ours makes more sense than theirs". Emphasising cultural differences and a hierarchy of rightness of cultures, swimming against the current, can result in rejection of the adopted culture and a failed immigration.

Cultivating an attitude of going with the flow, taking a mantra of "everything is welcome" allows a cultural adjustment to occur less painfully. In this case, Annabel starts to adapt to the casual nature of Australian culture, to learn what is humorous, appropriate or offensive.

Expats learn to embrace differences as the gifts of their untethered lives. As they go with the flow, they land back on the shore, intact but transformed, finding no exclusive cultures, but rather a mature and complex integration of cultures and beliefs.

There is another, essential expat theme in Annabel's story, the struggle of an expat from the "sandwich generation" – expats caring for their own villageless family AND worrying about ageing parents in their passport country. This theme will only become more prevalent as, worldwide, by the year 2050 the number of children will be exceeded by the rates of elderly. Not all expats' families will bless the move and, even if they do, there is always the pull of the needs of family in the passport country. This is an unavoidable conflict we must live with but also to reconcile within ourselves. We must accept again, those existential givens – the profound responsibility of our life choices which imbue our life stories with adventures and hardships – every decision represents an exclusion of other decisions, sometimes an exclusion of caring for family. Some expats bring their ageing parents with them. Others not only live with the guilt and anxiety of living far from ageing parents, they also sacrifice any semblance of a village they may have had to aid them in raising their children. The burden of guilt, anxiety or regret will be borne by the expat as will the journey to resolve those complicated feelings. If you can, make peace with your decision in your own mind, but also engage in open communication about this with your parents and siblings if you have them. Avoid seeing your dislocation as an all-or-nothing proposition: you can live abroad AND engage in frequent contact with your parents, both virtually and via visits. In fact, for many expats who do this, the relationship is often of a deeper quality with more frequent contact than may ever have been reached had they stayed nearby to their parents. On the other hand, you may also experience regret and guilt about your parents not seeing your children. There is no right or wrong answer to this dilemma, but each individual must face their decision and grapple with their conscience via an exploration of their own values and reasons for their expat journey.

Useful resources

Cloudstreet by Tim Winton

londonerinsydney.com

theaccidentalaustralian.com

CHAPTER
SIX

Restlessness, Rootlessness & Resilience

MORAG MAKEY
MATAPOURI (NEW ZEALAND)
& BARCELONA (SPAIN)

Morag Makey, 47
Matapouri, New Zealand

Photo by Pete Makey

Morag Makey is Australian by birth, British by marriage and Kiwi by choice. She has taken her three passports to multiple countries, creating and collecting memories along the way. In 2018 she co-founded IB Pathways, empowering students, teachers and schools in the International Baccalaureate programme. She describes her work as "the perfect intersection of education, wellbeing and global citizenship", three aspects that have defined her life so far. Morag is always ready for new adventures and prefers the challenge of the unknown to the predictability of the known, but she may have found in Barcelona, a place that gives her both and that she can finally call 'home'.

Restlessness, Rootlessness & Resilience

I never imagined a time when travel wouldn't be a possibility. For years, I have moved through airports with ease. Another plane to another place. Moving on for the next big adventure. An intermission with family and friends from my old life during my new life abroad. A weekend immersed in another culture to satisfy my need for 'newness'. Flights were booked, bags were packed and anticipation was high.

Then suddenly, without warning or preparation, we watched as borders closed, quarantine kicked in, and lockdown, isolation and face masks became the new normal. Travel within Europe was not completely out, but Australia and New Zealand wouldn't even accept my posted packages, let alone me.

With the possibility of 'home' removed, the pull became stronger, but with it, the question: what does home really mean?

I grew up in the far north of Australia, a small town girl, surrounded by people who loved life in the bush, particular kinds of expats, who had left cities and families down south to live life at the frontier. Maybe this is what gave me my thirst for travel. Some innate need for exploration? Or was it escape? Whatever it was, I was unusual among my friends. They were buying houses, having children and life in the same place stretched out before them. There was always a kind of claustrophobia in that for me and perhaps that is what propelled me.

It wasn't so much that I seized the opportunity to travel but that travel seized me. When I finished my Psychology degree, and the time for a Master's had come, someone mentioned teaching as an alternative and I found myself moving to the big city of Sydney at 22, to get my teaching qualification, my ticket to travel. That's how I have always referred to my degree, my passport to the world, and yet it was never a conscious decision. I often think back to my younger self and wonder how I was brave enough to leave home and why I have never returned.

After a year in Sydney, I never contemplated returning north and so began my mantra of moving on and never moving back, letting opportunities lead me and never stopping to wonder whether it was a good idea, or to consider how hard I might be making things for myself. The pull of familiarity was never as strong as the pull of the unknown, the mystery of the road.

At 24, I moved from Australia to New Zealand, my mother's story in reverse. I found myself in a place so geographically different to where I had grown up, suddenly surrounded by family I didn't know I had, in a culture that felt organic and gentle and safe. I can't say I found my independence in Auckland, because I had gone to boarding school aged 12, and my parents moved to Vietnam before my 18th birthday. I had been looking after myself for a long time already. But I think my time in New Zealand allowed me to find myself, or perhaps create myself, away from the confines of a small town, where my personality was shaped by my family, my school friends, and the shared history of a local community that at times felt stifling or daunting. There was always something in me that made me feel that I was on the outside, looking in. I had a sense of wanting to be part of things and yet not. Maybe I never felt good enough. Maybe I thought that if I stayed, I would have to compete to be extraordinary. Or maybe I felt different, a rare bird that was too noisy for the cage. I have never understood my compulsion to move, and to keep moving, only that it has governed all of my decisions, like an unseen puppeteer, creating a narrative that has revealed itself over time.

There have been many more moves since that first step across the Tasman, all of them haphazard: an offer of a job; a friend in need of a travel companion; a breakup sending me forward; an illness calling me back and, finally, a marriage that has created the most permanence in a timeline that is consistent only in its inconsistency. Leaving never felt very hard, because I was always so excited by what was waiting for me in the next place.

What felt hard, instead, was staying. Friends complained about scratched out addresses, updated too regularly to keep up with. Long before Marie Kondo helped us get our houses in order, my regular moves necessitated regular rationalisation for the things that would follow me to the next place. I have always looked forward to the process of stripping down, shedding and saving those few things that have travelled with me everywhere. And to starting again, a fresh canvas. The possibility of a new city, a new home, a new me. Although I refer to a kind of restlessness that has permeated my moves, that word seems to have a negative connotation, and constant change has generally only ever felt good.

In fact, after seven years living in Barcelona, my longest stay in one place since Darwin, despite loving our adopted home, that familiar feeling of itchy feet has returned. The future is calling again and the cycle of excitement, arrival, acclimatisation and normalisation has moved into that familiar phase of wondering. Who am I? What do I want? Where do I want to be? What's next?

It's hard to know how the lack of consistent roots has impacted on me over the years. I wonder whether my upbringing never felt very secure, and so I was always searching for something or someone that would feel safer. Or, whether my tenuous link to places and people made it easier each time to say goodbye, to move on and to start again.

What does rootlessness feel like? Sometimes, it's an incredible freedom from the constraints of a 'normal life'. It removes the competition for a bigger house, a newer car, a better job, a bigger pay packet. It takes away the need to play the game, because my game is a different one, that none of my friends and family are playing. I'm on the big adventure, after all.

Having no roots has created opportunities, or allowed me to take opportunities that many people can only dream of. When London became too big for me, a chance conversation at a yoga retreat in Mallorca became a six-month retreat of my own, living in a converted barn on a Spanish hillside, cooking for retreat guests, following the path of the moon each night and going to sleep with the sound of sheep bells, blissfully cut off from the world, immersed in nature and with the time and space to reflect on where I'd been and where I might want to go. That experience taught me to say yes without fear, knowing that things would somehow work out. It was also the start of my journey into Spanish language and culture, which resulted in my eventual move to Barcelona, via Argentina and Chile, a six-month solo trip that I still can't really believe I made; when I tell that story, it feels like it happened to another person, one much braver and stronger than I sometimes feel.

Because, despite the apparent fearlessness of a traveller, there is a certain loneliness and isolation. Sometimes, rootlessness can feel like being adrift at sea. Untethered. Blown by the wind, without a clear plan or a certain destination. But then again, doesn't mindfulness teach us it's all about the journey? Have I, in fact, discovered the secret to life? Minimal attachments, only the very necessary possessions (my ceramics collection notwithstanding) and a backpack full of memories, with multiple friendships in tow.

Yes, on my best days, I remind myself of those things. But being without a permanent home challenges my identity at times. Am I the girl from the bush, happiest camping under the stars in the Australian outback, listening to The Waifs? Or am I the Kiwi hippy, blissfully barefoot on Waiheke Island, with a soundtrack by Fat Freddy's Drop? At other times, standing on Waterloo Bridge, on my way to soak up the smells of Borough Market and the sights of the Tate Modern, surrounded by the music of London's traffic and a kettle drum busker on the bridge, I feel like there is nowhere else that swells my soul more. Until I return to Barcelona, where dogs and children and *abuelas* mingle in the plaza, with the sounds of buoyant and incessant chatter, and I wonder if another place could ever feel so good.

These sound like fabulous choices (and they are) and mostly I am grateful that I have been able to find a home, however temporary, in so many places, but there are times when I wonder what my travels have cost me. I distinctly remember the realisation that I would never again live in the same place as my brother, that we would never be able to meet for Friday drinks, or a Sunday barbie, or know the little details in each other's lives, limited to visits every few years, when time is spent filling in the gaps, or busily exploring the new location I am living in, and only really returning to just being as the trip draws to a close. We are getting better at that. I resist my urge to make constant plans while I'm in my hometown and we take our drinks onto the deck to watch a glorious Darwin sunset and listen to music and let the memories unfurl. But in the contentment of those moments there is always a niggling sensation that this is what I missed by leaving. The Welsh expression, Hiraeth, describes *"a combination of the homesickness, longing, nostalgia, and yearning, for a home that you cannot return to, no longer exists, or maybe never was"* and this has become a common sensation for me. Every time I am back in a place I used to live, or with people I have known but been apart from for years, I am hit with the feeling that I have given up so much by constantly moving.

Friendships are hard to maintain from a distance. Or sometimes, they can be built up to be closer and calmer than they are in person. Different time zones can challenge the less tech-savvy friends, preferences for the spoken versus the written word can allow the gap to widen into a gaping hole, conversations can occur at cross-purposes with misunderstandings that can't quickly be resolved or sometimes feel too hard to resolve for the sake of something that only exists in shared space once every few years. When important milestones are missed on either side of the globe, it can feel like you have been excluded, or they are not paying enough attention. When the little details are no longer shared, and the everyday becomes the once-a-year, it becomes harder to sustain what once sustained you. There is a kind of longing for the friend who once knew you without explanation, whose history was intertwined with yours, who hears that song from 1987 and remembers exactly where and who it takes you to. Yet, sometimes, when you meet that friend again, you realise that travel has changed you. You try not to talk too much about your weekends in Copenhagen or be so surprised that they have actually heard of pressed tin tiles in the design backwater that you assume you left them living in. You find yourself returning to conversations about the past, because your present reality seems so different.

That feeling of being an outsider, the very thing that nudged me onto the plane all those years ago, returns with a vengeance with each trip back to familiar places and people. Despite my claims that I am free from the comparison and competition of life achievements, insecurities surface when I return to a community of locals. When I sit on the deck of a friend's house, already paid off, the walls filled with photos of a life lived in one place, longing for that same sense of belonging. When we talk about our careers, hers at its peak after years of continual promotions, mine in a constant state of change, wondering if I could be where she is now if only I'd stayed. When I go with my brother to the local market of our university days, where Mary knows his soup order and asks after his kids, wistfully wishing I was known in that way. Or when I see friends gathering together for a wedding or birthday or New Year's Eve, dreaming of being surrounded by a big gaggle of friends, with shared histories and connected lives and stories that don't need to be told, because they have been lived together.

Yet, perhaps a traveller's life is viewed through rose-tinted glasses. When you go back for a holiday, you see the best in the place and the people. You remember the happiest days in your previous life. You forget the drudgery of getting up for the same old job each day, the wish that there was somewhere new to try for dinner on the weekend, the silent hope that your friends might talk about something new over coffee on Sunday. It's easy to remember the past as an idyllic existence, free from boredom, conflict or uncertainty. Of course, these things follow us wherever we go. As I said to a friend recently, I take me with me. But I am constantly evolving and learning and growing and filling that backpack with memories. For all the downsides of a rootless existence are all the lessons already learned and all the unknown stories waiting to be told.

What I have learned most from my travels is that I am a fixer. I like stepping into the unknown and finding a way to make it known, for me and for other people. In my career, I have always liked the challenge of something broken; an organisation without systems that needs a structure and a purpose; staff that need leadership and direction; students that need to feel understood and supported during their adolescent quest for their own identities. I like pulling things apart and putting them back together. Constantly starting again has made me good at this kind of jigsaw, with the resources and the resilience to take change in my stride.

When the world shut down because of Covid-19, my resilience came to the fore. While everyone else worried about uncertainty, I realised I have never lived with any certainty. My jobs, my homes, my lifestyle – they have always been temporary. There has always been a common thread running through them, that element of me that I take with me wherever I go, but just when things start to feel stable, it feels like time to move again. Constant change keeps me alive and has made me adaptable and flexible. I am not scared of starting again and I can live with a little chaos (although I do also have a huge desire to control my immediate surroundings, perhaps a by-product of having such a limited sphere of influence in places where I am not known). The challenges presented by Covid-19 and the changes necessitated by working from home, having less work, less money, fewer options; all of these are challenges I have faced again and again in my expat life.

More than anything, the vulnerability that Covid-19 created was a familiar feeling for me. Starting again so often means that you learn to open up quickly, tell the truth, ask for help. Reaching out to people is a common experience as an expat, because you spend your life holding onto the threads of friendships on different continents. Late night conversations and revelations on Facebook and FaceTime are the norm and doing this in lockdown was not a new skill to be learned, but a comfortable continuation of the way things have always had to be, the familiar territory of relationships in the expat existence.

Covid-19 also presented an opportunity for reinvention.

With the sense of freedom that comes from an expat life, not bound by societal norms, experimental, brave, open to new possibilities, able to live un-ensnared by life's trappings, the horizon provided a chance for change.

In my exploration of the concept of home, I decided I wanted to return to New Zealand, to my friends and *whanau*[1], where I believed my heart was most happy. The pull of *Pohutukawas*[2] and *Piwakawakas*[3], the flora and fauna of my adopted home country, became stronger with every day of lockdown and, suddenly, flipping my world on its head seemed in keeping with the world being flipped on its head. My ability to believe anything is possible, to bounce back, rebuild, start again anywhere, convinced me that the time had come to live my Waiheke Dream, to swim in the Pacific Ocean, under the Southern Cross. I felt that my soul would settle in New Zealand, that the constant wondering and wandering would cease. Instead, the card that I gave my husband in our first year of marriage rings ever more true: home is the person or place you want to return to, over and over. I feel lucky to have embraced so many people and places, for my restlessness and rootlessness to have given me such resilience. And to know that I have many homes, those I return to and those that I haven't known yet.

---

1. **Whanau:** Māori word for extended family
2. **Pohutukawas:** A New Zealand Christmas tree
3. **Piwakawakas:** A small insectivorous bird, the only species of fantail in New Zealand

REFLECTIONS

Restlessness, Rootlessness & Resilience

by MORAG MAKEY

It's easy to feel lost along the road less travelled, and it's tempting sometimes to look back, but there are so many things to be discovered and learnt along the way that make the journey worthwhile.

Understand your motivations for moving. For some people, the choice to keep moving feels absolutely right. Sometimes it is more of a compulsion than a choice. Try to explore who you are and why you are driven by the need for change. Examine which areas of your life need to change and whether moving is running to or from. I know that I need the stimulation of new places, people and experiences and that I'm not (yet) ready to settle. I also know that is not for everyone. The decision has to be about you, and your life goals, and what you will look back on, with a sense that it was right for you.

Sit still long enough to face the realities of your life. It is easy to keep moving and never really examine the elements that make up a fulfilling life. It is ok to want 'newness', but, can you also sit in stillness? Spend time exploring your values, your strengths and your ambitions. What makes you who you are? Who do you want to be?

Is there a disconnect between the different personas you represent in each place – the person you are now and the person you hope to become? Or, is there a common thread that connects you in each of these contexts? I worked with a Life Coach to explore my needs and that allowed me to move into a significant new life phase with a husband and stepchildren. When I was struggling to adapt to that new life, I revisited my coaching sessions. During lockdown in the Covid-19 pandemic, when my time of greatest questioning came, I accessed many online resources to explore my values and goals and I spent a lot of time journalling and reflecting to try to carve a new life out for myself. And I had a good therapist!

Work hard to maintain friendships and connections in your previous lives. I have always been an avid letter writer. I use letters as a form of journal, and my best memories of every place I have travelled or lived involve finding a local café or park and compiling a soundtrack of local music for my iPod, to soak up the place I am in and to share it with a good friend in another place. Giving friends and family an insight into my life helps reduce the gap that invariably grows the longer I am away. If they know a lot about my life already, then there is less detail to fill in when I return, and we can get on with the joy of just spending time together. I schedule regular FaceTime dates and I have some friends with whom I exchange journals – one of us will write for a month or two then post it to the other for their turn to write. With other friends, we have projects online – wellbeing challenges on Facebook, photo journals on Instagram, music playlists on Spotify. Each friend has a different preference for the frequency and format of communication and we find what works and adapt to what is going on in our lives at the time. And we try to be forgiving when things fall silent because life has a tendency to take over. Good friendships get through all that.

Give yourself credit for your bravery. I don't often think of myself as a risk-taker and yet every move I have made has involved incredible courage. It is important to reflect on this and to understand that there is a unique set of skills that comes with saying yes to things. When you write a CV, or promote yourself on LinkedIn, don't forget all the attributes you possess that allow you to move countries: creativity, courage, determination, resilience, self-reliance, independence, organisation. The capacity to leap should not be underestimated.

Appreciate all the things you've gained by moving. I have spent a lot of time comparing myself to people who have stayed in one place, and wishing I had accumulated all the things they have. I'm trying more to view my life through their eyes, and add up all the amazing experiences I have been able to have. It's not a competition or a race and there isn't one formula for everyone. This is my formula and it works for me and I have so many things that I would never have experienced and people I would never have met without all the times I've moved country. Yes, I've left things behind and I haven't had a chance to acquire certain things, but I have so many things in their place. I try, more and more, to record my reflections in a journal, to write about the things I see and do, so that I can look back over the years and remember all the little things that have made up my life.

WHAT THE EXPERT SAYS

Restlessness, Rootlessness & Resilience

by LEIGH MATTHEWS

In this bittersweet chapter, we encounter a deep dive into the philosophical marrow of expat life. Morag writes: *"Despite the apparent fearlessness of a traveller, there is a certain loneliness and isolation. Sometimes, rootlessness can feel like being adrift at sea. Untethered. Blown by the wind, without a clear plan or a certain destination."*

The expats journey is an existential one. Weight is synonymous with 'normal' life – the tick-the-box life of house, job, kids, family, one life, one identity and one country. Lightness, in contrast, the expat choice, involves foregoing fixed meaning and living moment to moment. Lifelong sojourners, without roots, become skilled carriers of this unbearable lightness which might be, as Morag asks, the *"secret to life"*.

The eternal outlander lives on the side of the sweet and unbearable lightness of endless polarities: opportunities vs roots; mystery vs familiarity; moving vs returning; freedom vs constraint; chaos vs certainty; flexibility vs stability; experimentation vs normality; ambiguity vs clarity; bravery vs fear. Morag's story is richly marbled with the vocabulary of polarity, the paradoxes and impossible choices of the well-lived life, which is not an easy life.

Home, in this global life, is not a fixed place; it is

a shifting concept explored through movement and adventure. Wherever you go through your life, there you are, and as you move, adventure, excitement, mystery, possibility and freedom move with you – the expat life IS a moveable feast. Home is a moveable feast. Morag exemplifies the way in which expat life revokes the very idea of place as determining belonging. Travel to other selves accompanies travel to other places, and the seasoned expat is capable of embracing this blind yet delicious unknowing and unfolding of self and place.

Expat life is a true reckoning with our existential givens – freedom and associated responsibility, isolation, death and meaning. Unwittingly, expats encounter these existential givens on a frequent basis, experience existential angst and, through these reckonings, come to be enfolded by the limitless possibilities in life and the changing nature of meaning and identity. They experience millions of deaths of selves attached to places, friendships fallen by the wayside, missed opportunities and alternate realities.

Morag's narrative illustrates the expat talent for sitting with yet another polarity: the riches and the costs of life unanchored to place. This is the paradox of life itself – with freedom comes choice, comes responsibility – the lead weight of lightness we must carry in our freedom. Freedom can lead to despair and regret and it does, at times, but it also leads to the love of the journey. In the love of the journey comes the cultivation of expat adaptability, flexibility, bravery, reinvention and resilience. In expat land, "home" is not a place, it is something without a fixed meaning, it is a thing, a concept, a feeling, whatever any individual sojourner deems it to be. Expats don't 'have' a home, they endlessly 'explore' the concept of home. What home is will shift as that individual shifts through life. Indeed, home can be many things at once: we journey with Morag through her various homes: *"the person or place you want to return to, over and over"*; *"where [you believe your] heart [is] most happy"*; and then surrender to the truth of many expats *"to know that I have many homes, those I return to, and those that I haven't known yet"*.

Useful resources

Why You Are Australian: A Letter to My Children by Nikki Gemmell

Wabi Sabi by Beth Kempton

Happiness by Design: Finding Pleasure and Purpose in Everyday Life by Paul Dolan

The 6 Minute Diary

Positive Psychology: The Science of Well-Being by John Zelenski

theresehoyle.com

viacharacter.org

theschooloflife.com/thebookoflife

CHAPTER
SEVEN

Two-Dimensional Dreams Versus 3D Reality: Friendships & Loneliness in Rural Italy

ELIZABETH HEATH
UMBRIA (ITALY)

Elizabeth Heath, 54
At home, Allerona, Umbria

Photo by Serena Baglioni

Elizabeth Heath is an American-born writer, editor and mom. She mostly grew up in Florida, where she studied fine art, humanities and later, archaeology. Summer trips to Italy to work on archaeological digs led her to want to make a permanent move. In 2009, she traded traffic jams and strip malls for tractors and outdoor markets when she moved to a tiny hilltown near Orvieto, Italy and married a local son. Their daughter was born in 2011. Today, she writes about travel, life in Italy, health and wellness, all from her bucolic perch up on the hill. She does, however, encounter the occasional traffic jam – of a herd of passing sheep.

Two-Dimensional Dreams Versus 3D Reality: Friendships & Loneliness in Rural Italy

Like most expats who move abroad as a lifestyle choice, rather than out of necessity, I viewed Italy with rose-colored glasses. I had idealized what life here would be like, and I very much bought into the *Under the Tuscan Sun* version of Italy. My friend and I even jokingly named my adventure "Under the Allerona Moon" after the town I moved to.

I moved to Italy for love, at a moment when I was at an emotional, financial and professional crossroads. I was ready for a sea change and I was afraid that if I didn't leap, my life would look exactly the same in a year's time – and that possibility was more terrifying than any uncertainty I was walking into. 11 years later, I still feel I made the right decision. But the reality of life as a *straniera* (a foreigner) in Italy – as in most places, I suppose – is far less rosy than the dream. No less satisfying, ultimately, but just not in the way that I'd first imagined.

I use the analogy of the sunflowers. In my early days in Italy, I wrote a guest post for an expat blog where I gushed about how I never tired of drinking a glass of wine in a piazza, gazing at old buildings and driving past fields of sunflowers. I look back at it now and it sounds kind of silly.

When I moved to Italy, I moved to the Italy I'd

imagined – where happy Italians worked hard, played harder, and were imbued with a sense of *la dolce vita* to which Americans like me could only aspire. I was sure it would be the Italy I'd experienced on my many extended trips – that of big, drunken, laughter-filled dinners with new friends, of sweet old men flirting with me, of quirky charms, and of Italians themselves as cute, carefree caricatures.

But after 11 years here, the superficial Italy of my imaginings has been replaced with the real Italy, warts and all. Those big dinners don't happen so often when everyone is busy with work, kids and ageing parents. A lot of those flirty old men are just dirty old men. Those quirky charms are actually an infinitely frustrating bureaucracy. Those cute Italians are not puppies, and they're definitely not carefree. And the sunflowers? I know the ***hole who planted them, and he only did so to avoid paying property taxes on his land. The piazzas with wine, the old buildings, the sunflowers – they're all beautiful and I still appreciate them, but the backstory casts them all in a different light.

Thinking about it now, I imagined Italy in 2D – with length and width, but no depth. When I was still in the US and showing friends photos from my trips, Italy could remain flat, beautiful and uncomplicated. Even when I spoke daily with my Italian boyfriend (who would become my husband), *he* was two-dimensional – sweet, handsome and attentive during our hour-long Skype calls – as flat, beautiful and uncomplicated as the rest of the country. In him, and in the rest of Italy, I couldn't – or maybe I chose not to – discern trauma, childhood abuse, alcoholism, addiction, depression, illness. But guess what? Those cracks in the social fabric are just as much a part of life here as they are anywhere else in the world.

When I moved here, those 2D photos and computer screens quickly showed their three-dimensionality. As we had planned all along, my boyfriend became my husband shortly after I arrived in Italy. We had a civil ceremony within 90 days of my arrival, so that I could remain in the country after my tourist visa expired. Our big church wedding, which I referred to as the "dog and pony show" (an expression that is lost on Italians, by the way), happened a month or so later. So, my first months here were a whirlwind of wedding planning and organizing accommodations for family and friends.

Then, all of a sudden, the honeymoon was over – literally and figuratively. My husband went back to work just a few days after our wedding. My friends and family went home. And I was left on my own, wondering what I'd gotten myself into – although, in retrospect, I didn't even have the courage to ask myself that question, because asking it might have meant that I'd made the wrong decision. That too, was a terrifying proposition.

My Italian language skills, adequate to get me through rudimentary conversations and boozy dinners, withered when it came to day-to-day speaking. I'd get lost in conversations and, by the time I'd jumped the mental hurdles of translating, formulating a response, then translating that response into grade-school level Italian, the conversation had left me in the dust. I was scared to use the phone, particularly if I had to call a utility or anything involving the use of even marginally technical terms. Reporting an internet outage was my worst nightmare.

135

Throughout these months, which stretched into years, I still plodded onward, convinced that I knew what I was doing and that, by benefit of my college degrees, life experience and good ol' American ingenuity, I was maybe just a *wee* bit superior to my new neighbors. I still didn't speak the language well enough. I didn't understand the unspoken rules of Italian social conduct. I didn't know how much I didn't know. I made so many faux pas, more than I'll ever be aware of.

Piano piano – the Italian expression for "slowly but surely" – things started to improve. It took about three years for me to be able to follow a quick-moving discussion with several Italian speakers. *Three years.* I still miss things, but I'm not embarrassed to say "I don't understand" and ask them to rephrase. I no longer assume that I know better than everyone else in the room.

That's one of the most sobering, surprising things about being a foreigner in a new country. *It's humbling.* And being humble has never been my strong suit. But my move to Italy and my slow, slow journey into feeling like I belong here – and that's still a work in progress – made me realize how much I had to learn. I've always been an observant, intuitive person, but in some ways, I shut down that side of myself, maybe in my efforts to plough through and keep pretending I understood it all. Life in Italy finally taught me to shut my mouth, open my eyes and ears and soak up – osmosis-style – all those nuances that I would have never overlooked back when my life was taking place in English.

In recounting this history, it may sound like my husband wasn't a presence during my steep learning curve. That's not at all true. In fact, for much of the time, he was my only real friend in Italy. And that too, was part of the problem.

On the long list of things I wasn't prepared for in Italy, loneliness was at the top. My closest friends all lived far from me in the US, and even there, we were only able to get together once or twice a year. So I rationalized that being even farther away from them wouldn't feel all that different. But it did, and then some. And it wasn't just being so far from my friends, who were no longer just a phone call away, but at least six hours and a really expensive phone call away. It was being away from my American culture. It's easy to joke about US culture as an oxymoron – we're a nascent country with the original melting pot of cultures and a tendency to appropriate the things we like. But there's a sense of humor, a sense of openness – at least there was before the Trump years – and a "get 'er done" attitude in America that is pervasive. So not only did I leave behind friends and family, I left behind 40-odd years of inside jokes, pop culture references and funny or fitting expressions that meant nothing in my new home, and just a whole different way of communicating and interacting with friends, acquaintances and strangers.

So not surprisingly, I suppose, I slowly filled that communication gulf with other English-speaking friends. As anyone who's ever moved abroad knows, expats are kind of like the Mafia – like secret handshakes, they have their ways of finding one another. Whether in Facebook groups for expats in Italy or getting introduced over coffee or just overhearing mother-tongue English being spoken in a crowd, we're drawn to one another.

At first, it's natural to want to connect with other

English speakers simply because they speak English. But *piano piano*, you come to realize that just because you speak the same language doesn't necessarily mean you're going to be lifelong friends. Or friends at all – *and that's okay*. Some of the other expats I've met have become trusted friends, others are friends I occasionally see for lunch or a drink, and still more are people I wave at when I pass them on the street. With a few of them, I cut down a side street when I see them coming.

Today, I can count my close friends in Italy on one hand. Two of them are American. One of these two lives close enough that we see one another about once a month, though we talk on the phone at least once a week. The other lives about 90 minutes away, but we exchange often hilarious voice messages on a daily basis. We all get along because we speak the same language – literally and figuratively. It's not just a language we share, but the shared experiences of growing up in the US, moving to a foreign country, raising kids and being the *straniera* in a strange land.

I have Italian friends, though I admit that I don't feel as close with them as I do my American friends. These are women friends I'll meet for coffee or occasionally go out to dinner with, either as couples or when we leave our spouses at home for a rare girls' night out. These are women who grew up in the same town as my husband, and who've known him for a lot longer than I have. I feel comfortable, but a little guarded, around them. Maybe it's just my perception, but I always feel there's a wee bit of judgement when I share something about our homelife, like how I don't iron my daughter's school smocks or that I occasionally – okay, once a week – serve my family frozen pizza for dinner. Hey, at least I cook it first.

These are cultural differences that color my relationships with Italian friends, but just as much, these are differences due to our markedly dissimilar life experiences. In the small, rural town where I live, almost none of the women have gone to college – those who do tend not to come back to our town to live. The women who work do mostly domestic or service-sector jobs – housekeeper, babysitter, cook or waitperson. Some of them are housewives who've never worked outside the home. So I struggled to form deep friendships with these women not just because they're Italian, but because we have nothing in common.

Then, when I became pregnant with our daughter in 2011 – my first experience with pregnancy – it was like I suddenly joined a club. I now had a shared experience with which to relate to my Italian women friends – I even had more to talk about with my mother and sister-in-law. Pregnancy, birth and motherhood became our *lingua franca* – the life events we'd all been through and could talk about together. It made it easier to be friends when we had something – anything – in common.

When Naomi started preschool and, increasingly, grade school, I got to know the other moms from her class better. It's been easier to strike up friendships thanks to the WhatsApp parent groups we're all part of and again, we all speak in the common currency of homework, school strikes, pediatricians, and chicken pox. One of the moms, who's probably half my age and a world away from me in background, has become one of my closest 'mom' pals – and her imitation of my American accent when I speak Italian is both hilarious and spot-on.

My friendships in Italy are a bit compartmentalized, though maybe they would equally be if I'd stayed in the US. With my mom friends we talk about mom stuff, and with my American friends – most of whom are also writers – we talk work stuff. We also talk about our relationships, our frustrations with life in Italy, and about a lot of the things I could never discuss with my Italian friends in my small Italian town. If I ever said to any of them, for example, that my husband Paolo and I were going through a rough patch, that news would be all over town and would very likely make it all the way to my mother-in-law, a worrier by nature.

When I think about friendships, life and loneliness in Italy, I often ask myself what my life in the US would have looked like had I stayed. There are all sorts of variables I won't unpack here, but one thing is certain- if I'd chosen to remain in the US, my relationship with Paolo would have fizzled out. It simply would have been too hard to sustain long distance, especially if neither of us were ready to move. My work as a writer was always portable. Paolo's stonemasonry and construction business, which he's spent years building up, is not. While we may have loved one another, we've both agreed that our love would not have survived had there been no promise of us being together in the not-too-distant future.

So when I imagine what life would be like in the US, I imagine that I might have found a way to have a baby, hopefully by meeting the right partner – even if it wasn't Paolo. But were I still single, I would have tried anyway, either through adoption, an anonymous sperm donor or with an assist from a sympathetic male friend. But then what? There I'd be, a single mom, or even a married mom, with my best friends, sister and sister-in-law all living between 100 and 1000 miles away. They would have been unable to help me in any aspect of childcare – and even if they lived closer, they all worked, had families of their own and probably wouldn't have been willing or inclined to pitch in and help.

And beyond the absence of actual physical help with a baby, I would not have had an emotional support network on which I could have relied. My mother was already in the early stages of Alzheimer's and was living in assisted living with my dad. My friends with children already had theirs years before me, and others had no kids and very little interest in them. So where would I have turned? Probably to wine and depression.

I made a lot of sacrifices to move to Italy and be with Paolo. I made a lot of compromises, and I still do, every day. I miss my friends in the US terribly. When we do see each other – once a year, if we're lucky – those visits fill me with joy, breathe new life into me, and make me miss them even more once we've parted. But when I take stock of what I have here in Italy, and the life that only Italy could have provided me, my list of regrets is very short indeed. I have a beautiful daughter who I never thought I'd get to have. I have a loving, supportive husband – even if he drives me crazy much of the time. I have a mother-in-law who is as good as gold and who loves me, even if she loves my daughter more – fair enough. I have Italian cousins, aunts, a sister-in-law and yes, friends, who would drop what they're doing and come to my aid if I needed them. I have my American friends with whom I can talk about work, men, politics, diets, whatever I may not be able to talk about with other people in my orbit.

My dear sister and I speak on the phone nearly every day. These friendships and relationships are robust, and they sustain me when I feel lonely.

Practicing gratitude has never been a strength of mine – I've always tended to focus on what was absent from my life rather than taking stock of what I have. But my life here in Italy is full of abundance – an abundance of love, kindness, trust, and security. That includes financial security, the importance of which, as someone who's teetered on the brink of financial ruin, cannot be overstated.

Italy, and Paolo and his family, have been the providers of all that abundance. Yes, much of it Paolo and I have created on our own, through our hard work and cultivation of our common goals. But it all started with Italy. I bet it all on the slim odds that I would come here and marry into a family, a town, a country and a culture and that it might actually work.

It was a big gamble, and I hit the jackpot – not overnight, but I definitely hit it. Moving here and negotiating this life never felt particularly easy, partly because I so naively expected it to be a breeze. Sometimes, even several years into this adventure, I worried that I'd made the wrong decision. Yet here I am, happy most of the time, trying to remember to be thankful, marveling at the unexpected twists and turns of my life that got me where I am, and having difficulty imagining life looking any other way than exactly how it is, right now.

And I can finally speak Italian well enough so that when I tell a joke, I can stick the landing – most of the time at least.

REFLECTIONS

Two-Dimensional Dreams Versus 3D Reality: Friendships & Loneliness in Rural Italy

by ELIZABETH HEATH

Moving abroad, whether you do it alone or with family, is simultaneously joyous, exciting, adventurous, sad, lonely and frustrating. I certainly haven't figured it all out, but I have learned some things that can make adjusting to life in a new country a little bit easier.

Learn the language. This one seems like it should be fundamental. But in Italy, at least, way too many expats don't ever learn Italian sufficiently to function here, or at least to function smoothly. Especially if you move to a rural area, unless you've immigrated to another English-speaking country, odds are that it's going to be hard to function with only rudimentary language skills. It's delightful to fumble through a discussion in another language when you're at the bar or the local market, and you can laugh, gesture and make faces to help make yourself understood. Try doing that on the phone with the cable company, or the gas company, or when trying to make an appointment to get some important medical test run. If it means taking language classes, private lessons, or setting up a discussion group with locals – whatever it takes, invest the time, and if necessary, the money, to learn the local lingo.

Don't just stick to your own kind. See the item above. You can't learn the language of your new country if you speak English all day long. This is understandably more challenging for couples, who speak English to one another all the time. But the end result is that you won't sufficiently learn the new language. And beyond the language skills, you can't integrate fully with your new community if you can't communicate with the people who live there. Sure, you can get away with just exchanging polite greetings with your neighbours. But is that what you immigrated for? Everyone has their motives, but for myself and many other expats I know, we left our home countries in search of a greater sense of community and belonging. But, unless you're willing to socialise with the people in your new community, invite them to dinner and accept invitations, participate in community events and lend a hand where possible, you're never really going to integrate.

Don't expect your new country or culture to accommodate you. Whatever you're used to things being like in your home country, suspend those expectations. It might be that your new country has different concepts of customer service, of what the inside of a hospital should look like, of whether you can get free refills on your soft drinks or extra cheese on your pasta. Maybe things that are social norms at 'home' are considered rude in your new country, or vice versa. Your new country is not going to bend to accommodate you. Its government, social services and daily customs are all different from your home country. And you're the one who has to do the bending.

Don't try to change the culture. You moved to your new country because you love it, right? But after a while, you discover that there are many unlovable things about your new home. They may be small or large inequalities, daunting bureaucracy, double standards, sexism or racism – all of which certainly exist where I live. Tackle the problems that you have some control over, and lead by example. I'm raising my daughter to be independent, tolerant and accepting, and to recognise and speak up when she sees or is subjected to injustice. She sees me do the same. But what I can't control or change is how people in Italy do business, what time they eat, how complicated it is to get a driver's licence, or the exaggerated sense of the *bella figura* (essentially, saving face). I've had expat friends here – several of them have moved back home – who've railed against the systems and expected their complaints to yield some results. Yet the only results were their greater frustration and alienation, and a lot of annoyed or confused Italians in their wake.

Don't spend too much time waxing nostalgic. Yes, I miss Mexican food, TJMaxx and air conditioning, and my American friends and I will sometimes sigh longingly over the absence of these things in Italy. But expats who constantly wax nostalgic about how much more orderly, efficient, friendly, affordable, cleaner and less corrupt their home country is make me wonder why they left. And waxing nostalgic (which is really just a nice way of saying "complaining") has a snowball effect. It's way too easy to find yourself among a group of expats who are condemning just about everything about the place they live – from how the locals drive, dress, smoke, drink, eat, probably even how they have sex. By doing the group lament, expats put even more space, more "otherness" between themselves and their adopted countrymen and women. It's negative, isolating and completely counter to their presumed mission of feeling happier and more at home in their new country.

Two-Dimensional Dreams Versus 3D Reality: Friendships & Loneliness in Rural Italy

by LEIGH MATTHEWS

Disillusioned *adjective*: disappointed in someone or something that one discovers to be less good than one had believed

Some think of expatriation as an escape, but escaping implies moving to someplace better. In many ways the chosen destinations of our expat hearts ARE better than where we were, but not for the reasons we initially thought they would be. Expatriation is a u-curve shaped story.

The Honeymoon. We start off like Elizabeth, on the high point of illusion with rose-coloured glasses, vacation memories, stills from films, a suitcase full of stereotypes and clichés wrapped up in naivete. That high point is the *la vie en rose* where we are living the life we had imagined. The Italy of sunflower fields forever, wine in plazas, art and history. The Spain of flamenco, tapas, Picasso and sun-soaked lazy Mediterranean playas. The Bali of paradise, lush green rice terraces, spiritual awakenings, yoga and massages. Our Instagram country, the postcard country, that two-dimensional country carries us through for a few idyllic months.

Culture Shock. When the high point bottoms out and sh*t gets real. THIS is expat life stripped bare. Read subreddits on the topic of hating Italy or Spain or [insert country here] to discover the verbiage of culture shock. The joys of pasta in Italy convert into a hatred of *"overprocessed flour in 100 shapes"*. Spain's siesta gives way to the inconvenience of closed shop fronts from 2pm to 5pm. Lost in antiquated bureaucratic systems, language barriers and cultural faux pas, expat isolation sediments. Your new country, your new life has abrasive and caustic dimensions you hadn't fathomed before.

Your unsinkable Titanic filled with dreams strikes the depths of a cultural iceberg and starts to descend with the weight of deeper, unspoken, unfamiliar and irritating cultural values that violate those you've long embraced. Time is regarded differently. Women are treated differently. Honesty is culturally relative. Customer service may be foreign here. Social etiquette is a complex set of secret rules. *Everything* feels different. There's hardly a ledge of familiarity or comfort to cling to. You've stopped #LivingTheDream and encountered the reality in all three of its harrowing dimensions.

Cultural Adjustment. *Piano piano* in Italian, *poco a poco* in Spanish, *pas a pas* in French, 'step by step' in English. It takes time, patience, a slowly burgeoning flexibility, the replacement of cliché with curiosity, and dreams with difference. This is when the breadth of the reality of your new life, a new culture, starts to feel more bearable, more understandable. You start to find a tribe and the language flows a little more easily.

Cultural Adaptation. This is the place where you are *"happy most of the time,"* as Elizabeth confesses.

148

Adaptation is a hard-earned understanding of culture and place, embodied by the greater ease that comes from developing cultural competence. You come to find peace in appreciating that there is no right or wrong, just different ways of being and doing. You take what you need or want and leave what you don't in peace.

The radical acceptance of things as they are also applies to the illusion of how life could have been had we not left our passport country. Perhaps the emotional support network we regret leaving would not have been there given that your people there are time poor. Perhaps the village that might have raised your children in your passport country is just the bare bones of sparse help too. Cultural values we held unquestioned become the subjects of deeper reflection. The amazing customer service belies a sinister cultural value that prioritises work over life and conflates being with doing. Perhaps punctuality is actually a time pressured love of productivity for profit.

We release illusions that protect our regrets and comparisons. We lean into what is and forget what should be or could have been. You've finally come to understand. Now you tell jokes about your two-dimensional dream in another language.

Useful resources

wantedinrome.com & wantedinmilan.com (news and information in English, plus insights into Italian culture)

anamericaninrome.com/wp (information about Italy, including learning the language and adjusting to life there)

thelocal.it (Italian news & views in English)

CHAPTER
EIGHT

Grief, Emotional Baggage & Belonging(s)

CARRIE FRAIS
BARCELONA (SPAIN)

Carrie Frais, 50
At home, Cabrils, Barcelona

Photo by Poppy Maidment

Carrie Frais is a British broadcast journalist and PR consultant who has been living in Barcelona on a permanent basis since 2006. In 2008, she founded MumAbroad.com, one of Europe's leading websites for international families living in Spain, France, Italy or Germany. She is also one of the founding members of Bremain in Spain, which campaigns to protect the rights of British citizens living in Spain and Europe, and hosts a weekly radio show and podcast 'The Soundtrack to My Life'. She lives with her husband Tom, two children Poppy and Bertie, dog Reggie and two cats Wally and Maggie on the outskirts of Barcelona City and is happiest with a glass of *vino tinto* after a day hiking in the hills.

Grief, Emotional Baggage
& Belonging(s)

January 2014

A sunny Wednesday morning in Barcelona. I am working at home. I see the word 'Dad' flash up silently on my phone next to my laptop. I immediately know something is wrong. I look at the screen for those few seconds before my life changes forever. When he tells me the news, in between heavy sobs, I repeat over and over how sorry I am, in the desperate hope that this could be someone else's story. Hands shaking, I call my brother. He doesn`t pick up. On a work trip to Asia, he gets to have a bonus night's sleep of *not knowing*. On autopilot, I call my husband and some friends. I can't remember how many. Some of them cry. I don't. I am in shock.

A plane ticket to London is booked. I throw some clothes into a suitcase. Something for a funeral. My husband takes me to the airport. We sit mostly in silence.

My mother is dead.

At the airport, the adrenalin kicks in. Heart pounding, I go through the motions of getting through security and to my seat. The safety announcements and chatter of other passengers are drowned out by my jumbled thoughts. Ironically, it is the first time that I have travelled on a non-budget airline on this regular trip, but the in-flight meal remains unopened.

An interminable plane journey. My stomach is tight. My heart continues to race. I rue missed calls and conversations that were cut short. I scribble down a few anecdotes for the funeral in a notebook. I try to remember the last words my mum said to me. I can't remember them.

I am desperate to see my dad, but also fearful. I know that, on seeing his face, it is going to make everything real.

He is waiting for me at one of Heathrow's arrival gates. Flanked by two neighbours, his face is pallid and drawn after a day he could never have imagined. I briefly clock the excited expressions of fellow travellers as they are greeted by loved ones. The four of us travel back in slow, rush hour traffic to my parents' house. It is pouring with rain. As we rush inside I notice that my mother's car has a smashed window on the driver's side.

I find comfort in the familiarity of being inside my childhood home, but I am acutely aware of my mother's absence. It feels surreal. My dad and I talk, including the trivial, trying to muffle the eerie silence around us. He tells me that, when identifying my mother's body at the hospital, she looked as beautiful as the day he met her. I am living through that day I had always dreaded.

I see a birthday card half written in her familiar sloped handwriting on the grand piano. Next to it, the remnants of a mug of strong, black, sweet coffee sitting atop a Bridge scorecard and a small translucent blue plastic bag labelled with my mum's name. Inside is a signet ring, a pair of broken spectacles and a watch.

In the days that follow, I spend exhausting hours on

the phone. I help organise the funeral. I clear out my mother's clothes and belongings, an impossible task for my dad.

I clean up the fragments of glass from inside my mother's car.

I spend the little downtime I have hunched up with my back against the living room radiator, sipping sweet tea.

My brother comes to the house. A face full of love and sadness. I finally cry.

January 2010

I travel to London with my family for a friend's birthday party. My mum picks us up after we arrive on the last plane to London, a trip she had made on many occasions. As we drive down the motorway, she clenches her fists in and out and I notice that she is unable to grip the steering wheel well. She mumbles something about it being due to the effect of the unseasonably cold weather, making light of something which turned out to be far more serious. Two days later she is unconscious in hospital. She has lost her memory, unable to recognise me or answer questions about who she was, where she lived, even the chemical symbol for gold FFS. She goes cold turkey, shaking violently without her daily nicotine fix. Doctors diagnose an 'unknown' virus. During her recovery, she temporarily develops a facial palsy, only able to drink via a straw. One afternoon, tears stream down her cheeks but she remains expressionless. I had never seen her cry. I stay at my parents' house with my two children, then aged one and two, until I am sure she will recover.

August 2017

We're all back for a summer vacation. My dad is in good spirits. He's got a new girlfriend. His new-found culinary skills are fully displayed at a family BBQ in his garden. He's laughing a lot (at his own jokes).

During lunch he starts to choke. I get that *panicky* feeling again.

Someone performs the Heimlich manoeuvre. He cannot breathe well. We take him to hospital. Unable to give a diagnosis, the weekend medical team sends him back home. Months pass during which he continues to struggle to swallow but doctors are stumped. He is eventually told that he has oesophageal cancer.

A date is set for an operation to remove the tumour. I travel over, only to have it cancelled at the last minute. A new date is set. I travel over again. The operation is postponed. We wait. Several weeks. I am at his house when he is doubled over in pain at 3am. He spends six hours on a trolley in A&E alongside numerous other sick, mostly elderly patients. He finally has surgery in the Spring. We are told it went well.

In June, he celebrates his 80th birthday with close family, a low-key affair. He plays the piano and recites poetry.

A few weeks later, he starts to deteriorate. Again, he has problems swallowing and his weight plummets. In a soulless consultant's room, we are told that the cancer has returned and has spread to his liver.

He has a tube fitted to his stomach. A literal lifeline. Every evening he connects it to a machine which drip feeds him for seven hours whilst he 'sleeps'. Months of physical and emotional pain follow. I spend more time at 'home', away from 'home'. My kids see him for the last time on Christmas day. Despite evidently being in pain, he manages to crack some (bad) jokes.

One evening, he is desperate. Crying uncontrollably, he looks upwards and pleads to my mum to be with him. It is heartbreaking. *I feel helpless.*

A few weeks later, he talks to my brother and I about taking his own life. But it is clear that he still wants to live. He asks for one more summer.

He passes away in hospital in March 2019. My brother and I are with him.

The house

Two days after my dad's death, I go back to his house, my parent's house, dragging a suitcase from the tube in the drizzle. The living room is still a chaotic scene, left as it was when the ambulance arrived. I won`t go into that. I go upstairs to my dad's office and see that box files have been piled up on top of each other, carefully labelled. One reads: 'Happy times & not so happy times'. Inside, there are numerous musical scores and reams of pages of poetry, some his own, others carefully chosen, some typed, others handwritten. I put them in my suitcase.

Another trip to England a year later, to visit my parent's house for the last time. A home they had shared for nearly 50 years. I take a last look at everything before the clearance company begin their work. So much is a reminder and a reflection of who they were and what I am saying goodbye to: an eclectic array of vinyl albums, a chest of drawers packed with playing cards, a bright yellow 1960s cocktail shaker, the grand piano, countless books and the dust-covered bottles of wine they had kept to open for 'special occasions' (take note, everyone). I watch on as unwanted 70s furniture is casually tossed into a skip. They are doing their job, but it feels like a violation of my parents' past. Empty and soulless, the house is ready for new owners. I take a final look at what is left – the worn down carpets and the clattery sliding doors which had heralded the grand opening of many (slightly dodgy) childhood performances. From an upstairs window, I take in the familiar garden view, lovingly cultivated over nearly five decades. Two robins, the happy songbird messengers of those who have passed away, land on the fence. I feel overwhelmed by loss and nostalgia. How can I say goodbye to my childhood home, to lose the connection with what had always been my focal point in England? I am afraid to leave. Afraid of saying farewell for good.

~~~~~~~~~~~~~

My mum had suffered a heart attack in her parked car, just a few metres from her house. A passerby had smashed in the car window having seen her slumped over the steering wheel. 40 years of smoking, a penchant for neat whiskey and double cream (not together) and she still managed to make it to 74. A former chemistry teacher, she once 'joked' that she kept a cyanide pill in the medicine cupboard. She told us that she was going to take it at the earliest signs of dementia in a bid to a) not to have to face her mental and physical demise and b) prevent us from witnessing it. Philosophical and pragmatic, she had never wanted to be a burden. Friends of hers at the funeral tried to make me feel 'better' by telling me that "it was how she would have wanted to go" or words to that effect. I take some solace in knowing that it was probably true.

My mum was never the same after her illness. She struggled to face up to her physical limitations in the last four years of her life, more so because her mind was still razor sharp. Bereft of whiskey and fags, it was as if her rebellious streak had been cruelly taken away. This was a period of my life when I felt the distance between us more than ever.

My husband and I moved to Barcelona on a permanent basis in 2006, just before the birth of our daughter. In an embarrassingly un-environmentally friendly plane commute, we had spent three years prior to the move travelling to London from Barcelona for work. We had met after being strategically sat next to each other at a mutual friend's wedding and soon discovered that we had a passion for Spain and that we were both looking for adventure, as well as love. We were living in Barcelona within a year of meeting and were married within three. When I fell pregnant, we were faced with a major decision – which city, London or Barcelona, would become our home? For now, at least. Without a huge amount of agonising, we decided on the more challenging option. Not matching the typical expat demographic of retiree or contracted employee for an international firm, we were part of a growing number of 'lifestyle immigrants' actively choosing to set up businesses and to bring up a family in Spain. The first couple of years were not particularly easy. We knew few people, and would sometimes question our decision, especially seeing friends in London climb the career ladder and enjoy ready-made social lives, but deep down we knew that that life was not really for us. In time, we built up our own businesses, created networks and made lifelong friends. We had two children, both of whom were born in Barcelona, and added two cats, a dog and some chickens to the family. We bought our home, just outside Barcelona, 10 years after our move. We'd spend mornings walking in the mountains, afternoons lunching with friends and evenings enjoying the city we had fallen in love with. Life was good.

Then, life throws a curveball.

My mum's illness and her death were both so sudden that, looking back, I realize that it took me years to process what had happened. With my children still very young, a business to run and an often frantic domestic set up, the mental load was already weighing heavily. So, I must have unintentionally blocked it out. And, as I was so far away, I think that I felt a disconnection with my former life in London, as if time there had stood still. In the first year or so after my mum died, I would travel back to keep my dad company, to teach him some basic cooking skills, to show him how to use the washing machine (really) or simply just to watch TV together. "I wish you lived next door" he had said to me once.

Thankfully, there followed a brief period when my dad's life was back on track. He chose to reinvent himself, part ladies' man, part budding chef, part entrepreneur. It was a real joy to see him happy again.

And then, that that curveball hit again.

The last few months of my dad's life were the saddest I have ever known. A charismatic, gregarious man, who was always the centre of attention at parties and among family gatherings, he struggled to come to terms with his life coming to an end. I used to dread the jolly palliative nurse arriving at his house, when she would go through the same questions every time. Without fail, she would start every question with his name. "Roger, how are you feeling today?". "Roger, have you been feeling suicidal?" "Roger, are you afraid of death *at all*?" "I am dying to get there!" he'd answer. He couldn't resist.

Having worked in the world of pioneering medicine most of his life, he researched every trial available and the various advanced treatments in cancer therapies. Looking back, it was evidently a distraction. If my dad had adhered to his consultant's advice that he should instead be spending quality time with loved ones, it would mean that he had accepted his fate. He travelled to Málaga on four occasions to receive cryotherapy (the freezing of tumours) at a private clinic. I met him there for his penultimate session. It was a desperate few days. He mixed up appointments and lost his keys and wallet. He couldn't really hold a conversation. A few weeks later, the last time he went there, he took six sleeping pills. Not enough to kill himself but enough to make us all acutely aware of what he was going through.

In the months leading up to his death, I experienced an overload of emotions ranging from anger and anxiety to frustration and fear but I also developed a close connection with my dad that I had never really had previously. Deep down, we both knew that our time together was coming to an end, and sometimes we spent long periods of time saying nothing, content in each other's company.

In those last months, it became an extremely difficult juggling act to meet the different demands of work deadlines, family life and my dad's worsening illness. Work was generally conducted remotely on a laptop in airport lounges, hospital waiting rooms, tubes and trains and conversations with my family were snatched in between doctors' appointments.

After my stints in London, I would fly back to Barcelona laden with emotional baggage. Literally. I'd have suitcases stuffed with handwritten letters from friends, family and former boyfriends dating back years which represented a connection with my childhood. I brought back boxes of photos, a pair of my mother's worn out gardening gloves, her favourite lipstick, an empty perfume bottle.

Then there was the emotional baggage that I'd carry around in my head. The endless whirring of thoughts, conversations and memories. Sometimes I found being back in Barcelona a welcome escape and then at other times I would long to be back in my parent's house, surrounded by the familiar sights, smells and sounds of my childhood.

When my dad passed away, there was initially a sense of relief. His suffering was finally over. Those who have lost loved ones from a terminal illness will know that one starts to mourn their death in the weeks before they die. But I struggled to come to terms with being an adult orphan at a relatively young age and living abroad seemed to bring this life change into sharper focus.

Soon after my parent's house was sold, Covid-19 struck. I thought how 'lucky' it was that my parents were not having to live through it. My mum, who started her career as a research scientist, would probably have charged headfirst into the storm whilst my dad, a self-confessed hypochondriac no doubt would have holed himself up in a room until it was all over.

Many of us have felt isolated during the lockdowns, but the pandemic, coupled with all the Brexit shenanigans, seemed to make me feel more bereft and rootless than ever. I began to question everything. I felt guilty that I had moved to Spain in the first place. I had known that my parents were getting older and may need me at some point, but I had selfishly followed my own path, to another country. I felt a deep pang that my children would not have many memories of their grandparents. Living in different countries meant that the time we spent together had been intense but the time apart extensive.

I also questioned my sense of belonging. It was fragile. Was I feeling more vulnerable because I was living in another country, another culture? I live in a 'locals' village and whilst I might be able to competently order the ingredients for a Catalan *sopa de peix* from the fishmongers, I can't follow my grandmother's recipe like the locals do. I am and always will be an outsider. There will always be walls – social, economic and cultural. Would I constantly be trying to overcome them? A never-ending task *of trying to fit in.* Had I moved away from 'belonging' somewhere only to realise that then I needed it more than ever?

But then, isn't being an outsider and being open to challenges part of what made me move to Spain in the first place? To experience freedom away from the cultural boundaries of my upbringing and see things with fresh eyes? If I moved back to England would it ever be the same as before? Could I re-assimilate as if I had never left? I am different now, with an altered way of living, a lifestyle I would not be able to replicate anywhere else. My habits, my way of thinking, the way I see the world have all changed. Moving abroad, losing my parents and links to childhood have all been hugely transformative, presenting me with huge emotional and practical challenges. Overcoming these challenges, however, have helped build up my resilience and I now rarely 'sweat the small stuff'. I am also beginning to recognise that the solid roots my parents gave me meant that I had always felt safe, safe to (literally) fly in the face of convention and to embrace new opportunities. I am living this adventurous life *because of them*. A priceless gift.

I want to do that gift justice and continue to move forward, not back.

REFLECTIONS

Grief, Emotional Baggage & Belonging(s)

by CARRIE FRAIS

Losing one's parents is an earth-shattering, life-defining event for almost everyone, wherever you live. For me, living away from 'home' when my parents died meant having to fully accept and own the decision I made when I moved to Spain many years ago, bringing with it some painful truths. Here are a few things I have learnt along the way.

Make memories. It is true that one never really appreciates the value of someone until they are gone. Until the pandemic, many of us were 'on the go' constantly and, for some of us, 'busyness' is often a way of not allowing the truth of our lives catch up with us. I have always been busy, sometimes through necessity and sometimes by choice. During the period of my parents' illnesses and deaths, I didn't have the headspace to think about anything else aside from work, getting two young kids to and from nursery/school and domestic chores. I now rue the rushed phone calls with my parents and wish that I had spent more quality time with them in the years leading up to their deaths. So yes, you do not appreciate what you have until it is gone. The truth is, you knew what you had, you just never thought you'd lose it.

Build your new community. The closest friendships are often forged through modern rites of passage – the likes of school and university graduations, one's first job or having children. Giving birth away from the UK was a unique experience and created very special connections. The friends I made through motherhood have become my surrogate family and their support and practical help was immeasurable during the aftermath of my parents' deaths. Close expat friendships can be made outside of parenting circles of course, but sometimes it takes a bit of courage to take the first step. Sign up for a club, explore a hobby, volunteer, join an organisation or take language classes. Living away from your home country can be isolating, so creating close friendships can help you feel more part of a community and create that all important sense of belonging.

Try to open up. I felt very disconnected and isolated when I returned to Spain after the loss of my parents, especially after my dad died. I had a strong desire to be back in my native England, surrounded by people who had known me since my childhood and to be able to re-live memories of my own upbringing. At first, I found this difficult to express to people who had not known me for that long. I found it easier talking to those who didn't need to ask questions because they knew my parents and had shared childhood experiences. I don't particularly enjoy talking about myself and am aware that opening up has sometimes made me feel slightly vulnerable and anxious. Since losing my mum and dad, however, I realise that by sharing difficult thoughts, feelings, weaknesses and personal challenges is how true connections are made. By opening up, one makes one's outer world as similar to one's inner world as possible.

Ask about your parents' lives. The years seemed to fly by so quickly after I moved to Barcelona. I look back now and realise that I missed opportunities to ask my parents pertinent questions during the times we were together during their latter years. During the school holidays when the kids were small, I think of the many superficial conversations we had and wonder why I hadn't switched the topic of conversation to subjects with a bit more depth. The reality is, now my folks are no longer here, many of the stories I'd love to hear have gone with them. I wish that I had spent more time asking them questions that would explain events that had shaped them, important decisions they made and the key life lessons they had learned along the way. I think about my parents as younger people much more now than I did when they were alive. And, as many of their friends have also passed away, unfortunately many of my pending questions will probably never have answers.

Carpe Diem. It's a cliché of course, but clichés are clichés for a reason. Losing my parents was a wholly transformative life event and I am aware that things will never quite be the same. Some of the physical effects were expected – insomnia, loss of appetite and lethargy, but the psychological effects were more unpredictable. I have experienced a range of emotions including anger, sadness, anxiety, guilt, emptiness, regret and remorse. Losing my mother so suddenly and not being able to say goodbye was particularly traumatic. I did have a long goodbye with my dad but this was not at all easy either given his ill health and state of mind at the time. It feels like both were gone in a flash. I have come to terms with the fact that we can't go back to how things were. All we have is now.

"What day is it?" asked Pooh.
"It's today," squeaked Piglet.
"My favorite day," said Pooh.
A.A. Milne

WHAT THE EXPERT SAYS

Grief, Emotional Baggage & Belonging(s)

by LEIGH MATTHEWS

"Here's what I most want you to know: this really is as bad as you think."
Megan Devine

Every human comes into life to lose. Expat life is seasoned generously with grief and loss. Friends come and go in our transient international communities; leaving one's birth country is an amputation; the gift of new culture/s and place/s for your children is the loss of the transmission of the cultural values and rituals you grew up with; the uptake of the outsider identity is a shedding of another identity of belonging to place. Beyond this, there will be deaths of loved ones in our countries of origin. Then we will ask the question: did they remain behind or did we leave them behind?

Carrie's story brings us this relatable metaphor of emotional baggage – the turmoil of the intangible but immensely impactful dimensions of our lives as expats paralleling our physical adventures. The overarching nature of expat life is a grappling with, and transcendence of, life's polarities that come to the fore for those in the arena: happiness-sadness, love-loss, coming-going, leaving-arriving, belonging-individuating, roots-wings.

Among the many discomforts in this dislocated life there are, perhaps, none so discombobulating as the grief wreck that comes from losing our loved ones. Sharing stories of grief in our death-denying society is essential because we can feel as though we are alone when this experience arrives and becomes a part of the fabric of our own narrative, even as it feels as though something is irrevocably *torn* from that fabric.

Your grief, its intensity, how it unfolds, and its complexity will vary depending on the significance of the person you lose, the role they had in your life, and the quality and character of the relationship you had with them. It will differ depending on the suddenness of the loss or the protractedness of an illness, which will likely come with anticipatory grief. Regret is a common side to grief, amongst so many other feelings, and certainly for expats who have "left" their loved ones in their passport country.

But leaving our country of birth is not the same as the people in that country being gone. That is the labour of grief and yet another shift in identity we must manage – who am I without this person in the world? When parents die, we become the last frontier and seemingly forfeit our identity as someone's child. In an untethered life, if we have a relationship with our parent/s, they can be a beacon of our belonging, even if we are navigating away from them. When they die, that beacon is extinguished and dismantling a childhood home can feel like an emotional maceration, of being exposed to the harshest face of our existential givens: death, meaning, responsibility, isolation.

Grief is gruelling. It is as bad as you think, as Megan

Devine assures us and, with the usual complications brought forth by expat life. The coming and going between countries, the surreal nature of flights toward tragedy, the juggling of children and partners in your chosen country and death and dying in your passport country, which you thought wasn't home but suddenly becomes a losing of home all over again. To cope with grief it is important to meet grief for what it is: the other side of love. We will not "get over" our grief but we can learn to live with the physical absence of our loved one and continue a different form of relationship with them. Opening up to grief becomes a vehicle for opening up to life as a journey that is messy, imperfect and painful in addition to beautiful, loving and exciting.

Coming to terms with regret means coming to terms with how you make sense of the world and the values that have guided you toward decisions, like "leaving" your loved ones and your passport country. Understanding your values will help you to salve the pain of regret. In Carrie's case, she integrates her leaving home as an artefact of carrying a solid home base from her parents throughout her life, so that her roots rise up to her wings. "*I am living this adventurous life because of them,*" she declares triumphantly. And so she has found a place of peace in the realm of complicated life choices that have some painful consequences. She has met her regret with her values and in turn with understanding and compassion.

The truth is, the whole adventure of life is the adventure of accruing casualties: past lives, places we've moved on from, seasons of life that change, and versions of ourselves that transform. Choosing to move forward is a repetitive exile from what we have loved and who we have been. The art of grieving is to learn to invite these awkward feelings in, and integrate emotional transmutations and lessons into who we become as a part of the rich mosaic of life impelling us, as Carrie writes, to "*move forward, not back*". And so, when we invite in the complexity of grief, and learn to integrate and honour the people we have physically lost, we find that we transcend once again the polarity of here-there, presence-absence as we must so often in expat life.

Useful resources

It's OK That You're Not OK: Meeting Grief and Loss in a Culture That Doesn't Understand by Megan Devine

Bearing The Unbearable: Love, Loss & the Heartbreaking Path of Grief by Joanne Cacciatore

Yoga With Adriene

therapyinbarcelona.com (online & offline specialists in expat challenges)

CHAPTER
NINE

Identity: Becoming Me (Again)

JANE MITCHELL
BARCELONA (SPAIN)

Jane Mitchell, 51
El Masnou, Barcelona

Photo by Maggie Michalowicz

Jane Mitchell has lived outside of the UK for almost 30 years and has a wealth of knowledge and experience as a mother, teacher, writer and designer living as a British expat. She lived and worked in Cairo for eight years before obtaining a PhD from The School of Oriental and African Studies (SOAS) on the Role of Women in Egyptian Films. Since 2003 she has been based in Catalonia, Spain. Jane is Associate Director of MumAbroad.com and is also an artisan quiltmaker with a passion for all things handmade. She lives with her three children and cat Morris in a village on the Maresme coast, just north of Barcelona City.

Identity: Becoming Me (Again)

"I won't be coming back". Those were the words my then husband said to me after months of us going around in circles trying to make our marriage work. If I am completely honest I already knew that, but hearing the words still floored me.

Eighteen years previously we had arrived in Barcelona on a new adventure. My ex-husband, an Italian by birth, had been offered a job which enabled him to escape a position that he disliked in Paris and I was moving on from a previous relationship. It was a fresh start for us both. We were young(ish) and optimistic about our future. I had a very fulfilling life: I had lived in Cairo for many years, had been teaching at The American University there, I was independent and doing a PhD, studying something I was passionate about.

The following year, our first child was born and I completed my PhD soon after. I debated whether to travel to London from Barcelona once a week to teach, to keep a foot in the door of academia but, at the time, it didn't seem worth it. Over the next six years I had two more children and a miscarriage early in my pregnancy. I found it difficult to tell people I had miscarried, given no-one even knew I was pregnant, so I relied on phone conversations with my mum for support. I worked for a while teaching English and then started doing research a few hours a week for MumAbroad.com, an online platform for parents from the international community living in Europe. I later became a shareholder in the company. I rekindled my love of design and textiles and sporadically made and sold quilts.

I saw my 'real' job, at that time, as a wife and mother. It wasn't what I had expected to be. Honestly, I don't really know what I had expected, but I turned out to be good at it and it made me happy. I had always preferred to follow my path as it was revealed to me rather than plan my future. Happiness has always been more important to me than having a successful career. My parents never actually said that to me, but it was certainly the vibe I picked up from them.

I feel a huge part of my identity stems from my upbringing and I subconsciously recreated the family life of my childhood – my father provided financially and my mother was a homemaker. The significant difference being that I had to face the challenges of living abroad and being away from my extended family.

I had left home at 18 to go to university and not really lived back with my parents since then, apart from during holidays. I had experienced life abroad in Cairo for a period of eight years before I relocated to Spain. There, it was sink or swim. There was no middle ground. I was thrown into a friendly mayhem like nothing I had experienced before. It was the most exhilarating time of my life. Losing a sense of certainty and control gives you a feeling of vulnerability but also gives you the freedom to be who you want to be. I spent most of my 20s in Cairo, arguably the most formative years of adult life, and that pivotal decade changed me forever. Living there gave me the opportunity to grow my identity in ways I had never expected.

I learnt the two crucial rules needed for driving – only look ahead and always give way to vehicles bigger than you – and I drove with confidence amongst the chaos. I taught Egyptian undergraduates eager to embrace western film culture. I fell in love with a man who understood where I came from but at the same time his upbringing in the Middle East was alien to me (his mother was English and his father had been Syrian). I met women who dressed in anything from skinny jeans and t-shirts to the *niqab*. I was fascinated by the elegant charm of downtown Cairo and the architecture that revealed decades of neglect. I travelled in the women-only carriages on the metro. I was as happy to eat *koshari* (Egypt's national dish), *foul* (Egyptian fava beans) and *ta'ameya* (Egyptian falafel) from a street vendor as I was to eat in a 5-star hotel.

My friends who were born there spoke at least two, if not three languages and had had rich, culturally diverse upbringings and many were in mixed marriages. As someone who hadn't lived outside the Midlands in the UK prior to living in Egypt, the expats I came across were equally as fascinating to me. Each and every one of them came with their own back story.

Living in Cairo meant finding a new balance: learning a new language, forming new friendships, adjusting to a different way and pace of life, understanding what a bureaucratic nightmare meant and accepting cultural differences. It taught me tolerance, acceptance, adaptability and an easy-going, open-mindedness that stays with me today.

So, on the surface, the move to Spain should have been much easier, right? Less of a culture shock for sure. But in reality, living away from my parents and three brothers at that stage of my life took on a different meaning. In Egypt I had been quite content being away from my family and going back to the UK for an extended visit each summer. But as soon as I fell pregnant with my first child I really missed my mum in particular and, after the birth of my daughter I realised that although it was my choice to live abroad, it was also a huge sacrifice to be away from family.

I didn't think it at the time, but when I look back now, I see that I am much more similar to my mum than I realised. The family values that I had, which were always there growing up and in young adulthood, came to the surface as I created a safe, warm and relaxed home environment for my own growing brood. I have a calm and easy-going manner, just like my mum, and I relied heavily on her from a distance. She was my 'go-to' person for anything baby or child related – and still is.

For the logistics and practicalities of daily life my ex-husband and I relied on each other – we were a good team. And if we needed backup, friends stepped in or we paid for help at home.

Being a full-time homemaker brought huge benefits to our family. It meant that I could be at home with each of our children when they were babies, look after them if they needed to stay home from school and allowed my ex-husband to easily keep his work commitments – long hours in the office and travelling. It also gave me the opportunity to take our children to England and Italy each year for extended periods of time. Our household was bilingual English/Italian and any babysitters we had were Spanish-speaking. My ex-husband and I both introduced customs, traditions and eating habits from our home countries. But nothing would beat a full immersion in good, old fashioned, family time spent with grandparents, aunts and uncles, cousins and family friends when we could be immersed in the language and culture and which we all revelled in during our extended summer trips.

We created a home that was a mixture of both our cultures. Some aspects of Spanish culture we embraced too (long leisurely Sunday lunches, local *fiestas*, school camps for the children from a young age and siestas) and others we struggled to see the logic of (routinely piercing the ears of baby girls when they are newborn, young children staying up very late and the battery of paperwork needed to apply for any official document).

Some customs we simply couldn't fit in to our lives. In Spain *Los Reyes Magos* (The Three Kings) play a similar role to Father Christmas bringing gifts to children the night before, or on the morning of the Epiphany, January 6th. However, by early January, the festive season was over for us. *Santa Lucia* had already done a detour of her normal route over the north of Italy and brought presents to our children on the eve of December 13th, and Father Christmas brought a second round. There wasn't space for every tradition from the three countries combined so we chose what we felt suited us best as a family.

It is an act of balance that I pass on to my children who are growing up as individuals immersed in a multicultural environment, who will hopefully be able to tackle life's challenges, assimilating competences from several cultures. They will build relationships based on all of the cultures they interact with. I often wonder which traditions my children will most identify with and will pass down to their own children, if they choose to have them.

Prior to my divorce, my life had been to create a home which combined two cultures on the inside (British/Italian) and two different cultures on the outside (Spanish/Catalan), so looking back I can see why I defined myself by my relationship with the people closest to me – my husband and children. My role provided both the definition and also the limitations of my identity. My family are the centre of my life but I was, and am, so much more than a wife and a mother. I seemed to have forgotten that. Couple's therapy ironically didn't save my marriage but it did teach me a huge amount about myself. My strength had become my weakness. Constantly caring for other people had meant rarely putting myself first and I had lost sight of who I was.

I've lost count of the number of times I introduced myself as being married to an Italian, as if that was the most interesting thing about me. But now I'm divorced what do I say? Who am I now?

I am a fighter.

I am a mother.

I am an academic.

I am an eternal student.

I am a maker of quilts.

I am a business owner.

I am a loyal friend.

I am a homemaker.

I am a listener.

I am a sister missing her brothers.

I am an alternative absentee aunt to my nephews.

I am a daughter grieving for her father and wishing she lived closer to her mother.

I am striving constantly to face the challenges of life in a foreign country.

I've been those things for many years, yet while I was married I validated myself through my partner. I think it is inevitable in a marriage to lose part of one's identity. Even more so when your partner is from another country and also when living away from home, when you rely on each other more. I believe that my identity became watered down as I adapted to both my husband's and my adopted country's culture and traditions. I think it is very rare to feel totally at home in a foreign country, however hard one tries to assimilate the culture and integrate. I think that, in my case, this led to a relationship where decisions were made based on the wellbeing of us as a couple and the family rather than decisions I made to further my career and personal development.

Despite my divorce and the soul searching that followed, I would not change the years since my children were born. I gave my children everything my mother gave me, in particular time, and I don't regret it for a minute. Why then do I still struggle to validate myself? Because I don't have a career or a traditional CV?

Is this a judgement by society or is it a struggle only within myself? If I think about it, I have not been judged in the slightest by the people around me. Maybe that is because we are all in this together? Typically, when living abroad with no family close by, your friends become your surrogate family and support network, bonded together by shared experiences.

We have built up a resilience by the very nature of having moved abroad and we often have an ability to adapt to the challenges and set-backs life throws at us.

We share unique challenges living outside of our home country. When one of us has a problem, we just 'get it'.

As a first-time mother in a foreign country, finding my tribe was essential. Sixteen years ago, I didn't know anyone else who was pregnant and there wasn't the plethora of Facebook or WhatsApp groups in which to ask other parents for advice. I had to actively find women with whom to share my parenting journey. That tribe has changed over the years as my children have grown and my needs have changed. When my marriage ended and I was facing my most difficult challenge yet, once again I found myself surrounded by a posse of amazing women. Women I admire, women I aspire to be like, women who understand me, women who support me, women who teach me, and also women who learn from me.

Some of them have been in my life since school and university, but most I have met since I moved to Barcelona. Some are my family and some have entered my life in the past couple of years. What is the common denominator? They all see something special in me. I see the extraordinary in the ordinary women I know and they see that in me. Most importantly we respect our differences and build relationships over shared experiences.

The prominent structure that defined my life has gone. It has been my girlfriends who have forced me to see myself in a different light. They had always seen me as an individual and not just as part of a couple. I have started to see myself through their eyes. The things that I thought weren't enough are actually what makes me, me. Now it is time to embrace them. Now I see that being a homemaker was not a loss of identity, but an integral part of my developing identity.

Certain aspects of one's identity are often suppressed in a relationship, perhaps more acutely when living away from home, but I existed before my marriage and that person is still here. Following a major relationship change one has the opportunity to become someone new or to find one's authentic self. I realise now that I don't need to change – I just need to bring to the fore all the things that have been latent for the past 16 years.

I have dyed my hair for as long as I can remember. Originally because I wanted to be a redhead and for the past 10 years to cover up the ubiquitous grey. I have been wondering what my now natural colour is for years. Lockdown presented the perfect opportunity to find out.

Taking the first step was daunting – not knowing what it would look like or what others would think. There are so many negative connotations about grey hair on women. Whereas silver-haired men are often regarded as sophisticated, women are frequently seen as old, frumpy or having giving up on their appearance. But I found myself inspired by the beautiful and inclusive community of #grombre (a play on 'ombré', a trend in hair colour with a demarcated line between two colours - in this case, grey is one of the colours). And I particularly love the trending hashtag #silversisters.

I knew that my hair would not change overnight and I knew the journey would be more important than the destination. Growing out my dyed hair comes in waves of uncertainty, confidence and acceptance – the perfect metaphor for this period of my life. It's a journey of being unapologetic and embracing one's authenticity.

Not too long ago being a middle-aged woman meant disappearing from sight, but not anymore. Divorce, bereavement, living with teens and empty nest syndrome – the challenging events of these years – should be embraced as part of our changing identities. As David Bowie succinctly said, *"Ageing is an extraordinary process where you become the person you always should have been"*.

Many people ask if I would consider going back to the UK now. My answer is, not at the moment. It would at least mean that I wouldn't need to plan out my phone conversations before making a call, or where I understand every word around me without even thinking about it. A country which prides itself on good customer service would be a bonus (although, this has improved significantly in Spain over the last 10 years). But, I find it difficult to align my British nationality with the path of Brexit and, perhaps most significantly, my identity is intrinsically linked to being a mum, abroad. I was once a new mum away from home relying on other mothers to point me in the right direction. When MumAbroad readers ask about anything from maternity concerns to teenage education I am now the one giving the advice and, if I can't, I know someone who can.

There are limited opportunities for employment in Barcelona but that has helped contribute to the dynamic and enterprising spirit of the international community here. The ever-expanding network of women I know is one of mutual support and collaboration, not competition. By living in this melting pot, I will continue to create my own sense of community and fashion my sense of self.

Without a doubt this is the scariest time of my life but also a very exciting one as I carve out a new future for myself with a truly inspirational group of female friends supporting me. The loss of a sense of safety and certainty which I had felt for the length of my marriage has left me feeling vulnerable but now I see that the only limitations are the ones I set for myself. Now I take responsibility for my own identity and with that comes self-worth. I have come full circle and am rediscovering the person I was when I first ventured to live in Cairo nearly 30 years ago.

I am still mourning the loss of my family unit as I imagined it would be, but this doesn't need to last forever. The acceptance of my new situation is a work in progress and I do now sometimes ask myself whether my divorce may just be the making of me, as I continue to put down roots in this place I currently call 'home'.

REFLECTIONS

Identity: Becoming Me (Again)

by JANE MITCHELL

I can't say I'm happy that I got divorced, but the initial shock of finding myself on a new life trajectory has subsided and I'm now comfortable with my new independence. Midlife has taken on a new meaning. I'm constantly learning about myself and beginning to enjoy the journey.

Find your tribe. I would not have survived this period without the support of my 'tribe'. Living so far away from family I realised very early on in my relocation experience that it is essential to have like-minded people around you who have a similar lifestyle and who understand the trials and tribulations of living abroad. I established a close community of female friends when I had my first child. I relied on their support when I was married and I rely on them even more now that I am a single parent.

Ask for professional help. While we may find it easy to talk about our problems with our friends, many people would think twice before approaching a professional for help or guidance. A therapist won't give you the answers but they will help you untangle the mass of thoughts going around inside your head that you just can't get to grips with alone. They can help you to understand so much about yourself, why you are the person you are, why you have reacted in the way you have, to figure out that maybe that so called 'perfect' relationship was not actually perfect and they will also be able to guide you to find the right path forward. Yes, they cost money, and the first therapist you meet may not be the right match for you. But when you find one with whom you feel aligned (and that is important), it is an investment well worth making.

Be open. Sometimes talking to acquaintances and even strangers can be surprisingly therapeutic. When I was honest with others about the challenges I was facing, the way I was feeling, the reason why I had been slow to return an email etc, I was surprised to find quite often that the person I opened up to had been through a similar experience, or knew someone who had and gave me a valuable piece of advice. Don't be afraid to share your story. Or, quite simply, when someone asks you how you are, tell them you are having a tough time at that moment, without going into detail, and again you'll be pleasantly surprised how many people will sympathise with you or admit they too are not having a great day. You may find a fleeting moment of comfort in the fact that you are not alone or, even better, you may find you unexpectedly help someone else by lending them an ear.

Be positive. A therapist can guide you and friends can support you but at the end of the day it is you who has to take the first steps forward. You have to do the hard work yourself. That can all be made easier if you think positively about your new future.

Things happen for a reason, accept your new reality with time, even though it's difficult and eventually you will see the reason why life threw you a curveball. Take this as a time to reflect on what you didn't like about your life and this is the perfect time to make the changes you want to make. Life abroad can indeed be challenging but with the right attitude you can reap the many positive benefits it can offer.

Take control of your narrative. There is a saying, "life is 10% of what happens and 90% of how you react to it". We can't control or change what happens to us but we can decide how to respond to these things. You are the only one who can decide how to react to the challenges life throws at you. Once you accept that, your life becomes much easier, and for some, adversity is where they thrive.

WHAT THE EXPERT SAYS

Identity: Becoming Me (Again)

by LEIGH MATTHEWS

"Losing a sense of certainty and control gives you a feeling of vulnerability but also gives you the freedom to be who you want to be". Jane references her first expat stint in Cairo thus, but she could equally be writing about living the other themes woven throughout her expat story including Motherhood, divorce, sisterhood and identity.

Jane's story lays bare the full significance of being a (heterosexual CIS) woman on the expat journey. Trends may change, gender roles may shift, and not every expat woman chooses to have children but, the assumption of the role of Mother and Wife, and the laying aside of career aspirations and ourselves, is a frequent song of the expat woman. It is the common herstory of the expat wife that she will have had an identity formed in a full life prior to marriage – one of career, aspirations, passions and networks. Bold, carefree and self-determined, the enviable Independent Women of Destiny's Child, *"All the ladies who truly feel me throw your hands up at me!"*, who forsook that path for variations on the blog title *"What it's really like to give up everything and become an expat wife".*

Gender roles structure the opportunities and constraints that accumulate in any woman's life, but, the expat life itself implores someone to fill the vacuum where a village may have been to raise our children had we stayed in our passport lands. If one is an accompanying spouse, the laying down of oneself as the bridge between public and private for one's partner comes as an imperative as he flies from place to place, often leaving the expat woman not only village-less but also in the role of single parent each time he is away. Selflessness is not just socialised, it is also demanded by circumstances, and expat family life is a perfect storm in which to birth the Mother who sacrifices for her family. Jane, however, like many Mothers, carries her role with a grace, humility and gladness radiating from the understanding that there is no greater responsibility than that of Mothering humans and raising Third Culture Kids, our global citizens, no less. The anchoring power of the Mother in the provision of consistency, ritual and love in a life full of culture clashes and unknowns is critical. Yes, *"The frequency of the mother is the frequency of the world"* (@thermotherspirit).

Bafflingly, most societies do not respect the role of the Mother, expat or not. Less so does society respect the power of the ageing woman. @themotherspirit speaks to the slanted view of women in our latter life cycles:

"As maturing women we've been cultured... to shrivel and be brittle, break and disappear. It's as if ageing women are told to fade into invisibility but nature teaches us to mature to become our most visible, beautiful and alive – it is to ripen and radiate."

We strain under the dislocation from our Mothers as we ourselves become Mothers. There is an innate yearning for the transmission of wisdom and consolation, if your Mum is "that kind" of Mum. The notion of the village recedes and, in its place, we may find a network of sisters. *"Find your Tribe"* is a resonant chant of the veteran expat woman and it can be that the coming together of sisters in friendships constitute vigorous and vibrant threads stitched through an expat woman's journey. As SARK writes: *"The circles of women around us weave invisible nets of love that carry us when we are weak and sing with us when we are strong."*

When we look at, and to, our resilient expat sisters, when we read the stories in this book, we retrieve forgotten dimensions of ourselves. We meet again, the emboldened woman, embracing but transcending the selves built from the constraints and opportunities of gendered roles in our expat lives. As a maturing expat woman, Jane speaks inspiringly of emboldening the grey, reclaiming her identity beyond that of Mother and Expat Wife. She is casting off the cultural script of the valueless middle aged woman, and venturing forth beyond the borders of the marital relationship; becoming herself (again). In the uncertainty and loss of control she is indeed simultaneously vulnerable and free, revealing as, @themotherspirit declares: *"By midlife, women are not invisible. They have become invincible. This is your arrival."*

Useful resources

Mating in Captivity: Unlocking Erotic Intelligence by Esther Perel

mumabroad.com (relocation stories and living abroad experiences)

noon.org.uk (inspirational stories from women in midlife)

Lightning Source UK Ltd.
Milton Keynes UK
UKHW020718180921
390790UK00005B/413

9 781838 174675